ENDORSEMENTS

"*Think Differently Learn Differently* by Bob Hamp is a book that helps us drill deeper into understanding how successful relationships work. Bob is an effective trainer, counselor and teacher in the areas of relationships and personal freedom. I appreciate the exploration of brain science and its applications to love and connection. This book is a tool to help you understand yourself as well as those important relationships around you. If you are asking the question, "What book should I read next to help me grow in my impact and effectiveness in working with people?" then you just found it. I'd highly recommend that you read *Think Differently Learn Differently* to equip yourself as a leader, spouse, parent or friend."

Danny Silk
Author of *Keep Your Love On* & *Business of Honor*

"For business owners, ministry leaders, speakers, authors or just anyone who has a voice and a message to share, this is the book for you! Bob Hamp is a master communicator that invites you on a journey to not just be taught but to learn for yourself how to effectively communicate your message. Buy this book, read it, and apply it. Get your message out to all of us who need to hear it. He can and will help you."

Amy Ford
Co-Founder of Embrace Grace

"Bob Hamp has a unique ability to teach and communicate in such a way to produce life change. This book reflects Bob's heart to help all people learn how to be effective in reaching others with the truth and power of God's Word, thus bringing fresh revelation and newfound freedom in Christ."

Nancy Alcorn
Founder & President of Mercy Multiplied

"When Bob sent me the preliminary manuscript to what would become *"Think Differently Learn Differently,"* I expected nothing less than what I had experienced in his previous two books: a complete overhaul in my thinking. But what I found in this book moved me on a level that I could never have predicted. Contained in the pages of this book are answers to questions I didn't know to ask. *Think Differently Learn Differently* isn't just another logical offering in a chain of great "how to" guides. This book goes to the heart of how we hear, speak, learn, and change. And how we help others do the same. Read it slowly. Ponder it intentionally. The simple but overlooked truths you're about to discover will forever alter the way you interact with others and will immediately improve your learning."

Pastor Hart Ramsey
Senior Pastor, Northview Christian Church

"The power of communication is life changing and if life change is what you are after then you have found the right book. But don't open the pages of this book if you are only looking to change other's lives. Open these pages to change your own life first to become a powerful, congruent communicator from the inside out. This book isn't just about learning skills, it's about discovering the beauty of communicating with change in mind. Now grab a pen, take a deep breath and turn the page…your life is about to change!"

Polly Hamp
Author, Speaker & Think Differently Coach

"P.S. I have to share about how unbelievably proud I am of my husband for this book he has birthed. He is a brilliant writer, communicator & my best friend. He doesn't just help minds think differently, he speaks to hearts and loves extravagantly!"

"Bob Hamp is an incredible communicator who is dedicated to life-long learning. His insight into thinking, learning, leading and living differently have been transformative in my life, my family and friends lives', and I know in countless others. If you are wanting to be a true change-maker then read this book!"

Justin Wren
Humanitarian & MMA Heavyweight

"As a songwriter, my life is full of "why-didn't-I-think-of-that" moments, and this book is full of them too. Bob Hamp weaves elements of scripture, science, popular culture, and good old-fashioned logic to re-introduce us to our own minds. There's a simple brilliance to his perspectives, which will open your eyes to the profound possibilities within and before you, and prepare you for the wisdom that waits around the next corner."

Paul Duncan
Platinum-selling *songwriter*, Podcaster & Worship *leader*

"When was the last time you thought about how your mind works? Classroom effectiveness is lifeblood of any academic. This practical handbook shows leaders, teachers, ministers, counselors and professionals how to communicate with transformational power to enable change. Packed full of examples and strategies, *Think Differently Learn Differently* brings together a vast body of knowledge ranging from neuroscience to scripture. This is not a quick fix hack, but a deep dive into the DNA of why we respond the way we do to powerful communication."

Michael Winegeart
Executive Director, Spark: Lipscomb's Idea Center

"You owe it to yourself to read this book if you desire to be better equipped to connect with a patient, large group of people, your family, or simply the person across the table. Bob Hamp outlines and explores how we learn and communicate to one another. This book is an essential tool for doctors trying to help patients make holistic improvements in their lives."

Dr. James A. Palma, Jr., D.C.
Chiropractor

"I enjoy discovering books which validate me as a person or resonate emotionally with my own journey. Every now and again I read a work which challenges my paradigms and cracks open a genuinely new perspective. On even rarer occasions, I encounter a gem that brings clear articulation to instincts which previously had only nondescript language— it is extraordinary to find all these in one book. In *Think Differently Learn Differently*, Bob Hamp has provided speakers, teachers, and influencers with the Rosetta Stone to bridge head and heart in the practice of intentional, transformational communication."

Wendy K. Walters
Motivational Speaker & Master Coach

"TRANS[fer of in]FORMATION is easily confused with transformation. One increases knowledge; the other offers an experience the listener can engage with and be transformed by. My own life has been radically transformed by the power of the message contained in this book. I now use my experience of transformation in my life's work. I can offer no greater endorsement than that.
Think Differently Learn Differently is Bob Hamp's third book in a series. While this book will stand on its own, the message is most effectively received when progressively consumed in order, as intended by the author: Live, Lead, Learn."

Anna LeBaron
Author

THINK DIFFER ENTLY LEARN DIFFER ENTLY

Communication with Change in Mind

A book by
BOB HAMP

Think Differently Learn Differently
Communication with Change in Mind
Copyright © 2018 by Bob Hamp

The New Testament in Modern English by J.B. Phillips copyright © 1960, 1972 J. B. Phillips. Administered by The Archbishops' Council of the Church of England. Used by Permission.

ISBN: 978-1-5323-8941-2
Library of Congress Control Number:

Visit www.bobhamp.com for additional ministry information.

Cover & Layout Design by Scott Cornelius and ThinkTree Media

Printed in the USA

CONTENTS

DEDICATION

This book is dedicated to an unending line of teachers and friends who have changed my mind and changed my heart. Some of you came into my life to help me learn and grow, and some of you just helped me learn and grow by being in my life. My heart and mind is a synthesis of authors, teachers, counselors, editors, and friends who have shifted and stirred my mind—while touching and connecting to my heart.

This is also dedicated to my grandchildren and grandchildren to come. May they Learn Differently.

ACKNOWLEDGMENTS

Every book that becomes a book arises from a synthesis of learning and thinking in the context of the life of an author. It could almost be a recipe. This recipe has resulted for me in a third course to a meal that has lasted eight years as of the writing of this book. This course for me has been a delicious, slow-simmering entrée served by thinkers, teachers, rabbi's therapists in the the ever important dining room of people who love and support the craziness and fire that is authorship.

I cannot say enough about what it has been to write this book from a place of rest and peace. My first book was a rugged birthing process, and my second book was an outright war. This book was a sculpture allowed to evolve in the best possible studio, a place the heart calls "home."

Great thinkers and writers and communicators went on before me to allow me to make soup out of the sumptuous meat they had produced. From the founders of Neuro-Linguistic Programming to Neil Anderson, a grandfather to Freedom thinkers, I am grateful for people who take time to think about thinking and then commit these ideas to paper and sound.

In the process of creating a clean, clear manuscript every author must have an editor who makes him look good. I had two in the amazing husband and wife team of Chris and Gena Maselli who not only edited my book, but truly seemed to love my recipes and hand them back each time with the satisfied smile of people partnering in a dream.

Details are not always the language of writers so I am grateful for the proofreading work of Christina Farrah and Colette White who lovingly and eagerly cleaned up after me in the kitchen.

And helping serve the meal to the rest of the world, I am grateful for the book launching expertise and passion of Anna LeBaron.

And last, although first, I cannot say enough about my wife Polly. She gave nurture of soul and labor that allowed me to return again and again to the keyboard with full heart and full mind. She loved me and my book while it demanded my time, argued with my mind and held my attention for long periods of time. She loved the book with me and loved the process while contributing her own priceless thoughts and prose. In this book you will see hints of her everywhere even if you don't recognize it. She made me and this book better while it was prepared, simmered and cooked and filled our house with its fragrance for almost a year.

With a book, the old adage about too many cooks is seldom true. This book and my thinking is the synthesis of a whole team of people and I am deeply grateful to them all.

INTRODUCTION

Neo blinked, a dull pain pulsating through his skull. "Why do my eyes hurt?"

Morpheus leaned in. "You have never used them before."

This was a simple yet profound moment in the mind-shifting 1999 sci-fi classic movie *The Matrix*… and it's a conversation every student should have with their teacher on their journey of transformation.

Why do my eyes hurt?

In his late-20s, Neo believed he was living life as well as anyone else. He had a job, an apartment, and a social life. So when he discovered he had actually spent his life sealed in a pod—being fed virtual reality signals by an army of artificially intelligent machines—everything shifted.

But Neo didn't make the discovery on his own. His revelation only came because someone pulled his body from the machinery and forced him to open his eyes. Of course, it was too much to take in all at once. But as he lay on the table, squinting into the light, he asked the inevitable question, "Why do my eyes hurt?" Morpheus' veiled response, "You have never used them before," sparked both answer and mystery. The response, while succinct, only produced a seed of understanding. Actual understanding was yet to come.

When our goal in communication is to help people experience meaningful change, we must begin with the question: *In what way have they not used their eyes yet?*

Then we must set about opening them.

WELCOME TO THE REAL WORLD

Helping others open their eyes and discover meaningful change is what this book is all about. In my book, *Think Differently Live Differently: Keys to a Life of Freedom,* I talked about how to receive freedom. But once I finished writing that book, a nagging question begged to be answered:

Once you receive your freedom, how do you share the breakthrough you've received in a meaningful way that encourages understanding and a response in others? In other words, how do you help others receive that same freedom?

The answer to that question became clear—communication. Communication is the key to facilitating change in others. It's the key in helping them open their eyes and learn the truth, too.

In this book, *Think Differently Learn Differently,* you'll find answers to question such as:

- How does learning occur and what part does communication play in that process?

- What is the difference between covert and overt communication? And why does it matter?

- How are words and ideas connected?

- How are the left brain and the right brain different, how can you communicate effectively to both and why does this matters?

- Can lifelong mindsets change, and if so, what do people need to know in order to change theirs?

- What part does the Holy Spirit play in bringing about change—and how can you partner with Him to teach others?

- What tested techniques can you use to impact your audience to the highest degree?

If we shift the way we think about communication, we shift the way we communicate. If we shift the way we communicate, we shift the way our listeners or readers hear or read. If we shift the way they hear or read, then the transformation that follows is inevitable.

Of course, the change we seek is not for our own benefit, to move others to our way of thinking, or to manipulate them into doing something we want. While any tool can be used for manipulation, the models of change found in this book point people back to their truest selves. Behavioral change or a change of attitude is most powerful when it parallels a move toward discovery and reconnection with one's identity. That's the kind of change that allows others to finally break through barriers and find the lives they were meant to live.

Communication that fosters deep and meaningful change reaches across the chasm between two people. It targets the change residing inside the listener and grants them the opportunity to let it out.

This book will take elements of counseling and change theory and combine it with bits of brain science and Neuro-Linguistic Programming (NLP) to help you understand communication better. Add in elements of biblical truth and this book becomes a manual to help you use your language to move behind common human defenses. From there you can issue an invitation for people to fully become who God created them to be in the face of a lifetime of opposition.

Read slowly. Experiment with the techniques. Let the ideas simmer. Question some of your long-held assumptions. Whatever you do, do it *differently*. If you read this book with the intent of understanding how people learn and how you can communicate more effectively with them, then you—yourself— will begin to think differently, too.

To illustrate the powerful truths to come, let's begin our time together with the story of an old friend, one you probably remember if you have read my first book, *Think Differently Live Differently*—the acrobat who finds his true self. We won't revisit the acrobat's childhood in-depth. No, today, we'll continue his story. We'll learn what he discovers about learning and get a picture of what freedom looks like when it's passed on.

CHAPTER 1

LEARNING TO FLY (A PARABLE)

A soul in tension that's learning to fly /
Condition grounded but determined to try
—Pink Floyd, *Learning to Fly*

I can't just run off and join the circus.
—P. Carlyle, *The Greatest Showman*

The acrobat stood on a narrow stand at the top of a towering pole. He stared down at the audience below. Could he leave the only life he had ever known for the possibility of finding the life he had always dreamed of?

He was torn for only a moment.

With a deep breath, he took a step forward, reached out and grabbed the swing. The audience gasped.

This wasn't just any acrobat. And this wasn't just any performance. This young man was born to two beloved acrobats from a famous traveling troupe. Their hope had rested on his future, but sadly, within a month of his birth, he was tragically lost while the troupe traveled the back roads late one night.

Found by a hardhearted farmer and his anxious wife, the young man was raised as their own for the first 17 years of his life. The only life he knew was that of the farm and his new, fretful family. Still, an unrequited burning to defy gravity filled his chest. He had no way of knowing that the source of this yearning came from his true nature. He only knew to work the ground.

In his seventeenth year, he was restored to his family of birth and began his journey of overcoming the years of disconnection to become the young man he was created to be. He overcame lifelong mindsets and emotional barriers as well as physical limitations to finally release his true nature on the trapeze. Tonight his painstaking journey found expression in a jaw-dropping performance like the troupe of acrobats had never seen.

(See the full, original parable in my book, *Think Differently Live Differently*...you'll be glad you did as the details of the story take the reader through the journey of the human soul from the hope of original creation through a set of common barriers to an unleashed life of freedom. But for now, let's continue the acrobat's story...)

As his performance ended, the crowd was on its feet. Roars and cheers filled the tent! His heart bursting with emotion at his personal breakthrough and performance, he climbed down from the trapeze. He dismounted in the midst of young student acrobats who felt the adrenaline of watching a spectacular performance unlike anything they had ever thought possible.

TEACH US HOW TO DO THAT

"That was incredible!"

"Wait, how did you do that thing when...?"

"I can't believe you made the release!"

"How did you even come up with that twist thing?"

Then the voices that surrounded him began to arrive in a similar place.

"Can I do that?"

"Can you show me that dismount?"

"Will you show me how to do that first sequence?"

"Teach us!" several voices shouted.

"Yes, teach us!" they all agreed. They wanted nothing less than for him to help them also learn the kind of unfettered performance they had just witnessed.

Still laughing and catching his breath, he agreed.

"Let's meet, and I can show you what I know," he said, still on an adrenaline high. "It'll be a blast!"

The energy carried everyone through the rest of the afternoon and evening. As the acrobats all moved about their own business, they could still be heard marveling at the performance they had seen earlier that day. It had made a mark on them all.

THE LESSONS BEGIN

The day finally arrived for the acrobat to share his knowledge. The group of young acrobats chattered as they filed into the practice tent, now quiet and empty, eager to learn. They began recounting to one another what they had seen and firing questions at the acrobat.

He gathered them together and considered how to best teach them what he had done. He wasn't a seasoned instructor. The student acrobats already had plenty of those, and since he hadn't spent his life with the troupe's instructors, he didn't think in the same way as the rest of them anyway. He thought about things differently, from outside of the others' framework.

As he sat down with the students, he decided to begin with questions and conversation.

"What did you see that day?" he asked.

It quickly became clear that even though everyone had watched the same performance in the same place at the same time, they had each seen something very different. It was almost as if they were at different performances. Some of them even described things he was sure he had not done! Was it possible that each of them had a different way of seeing even though they had watched the same event?

> **"WAS IT POSSIBLE THAT EACH OF THEM HAD A DIFFERENT WAY OF SEEING EVEN THOUGH THEY HAD WATCHED THE SAME EVENT?"**

He then asked them, "What did you like the most?"

Again, they all described something different. Some of them liked this or that specific move. Some couldn't remember specifics at all, but they knew they had enjoyed the way they had felt while watching him.

His questions taught him much about the group. He learned not only what they wanted to learn, but he also began to learn who they were as individuals and what thrilled them.

When it came time to give step-by-step instructions, the acrobat asked his students to watch his routine again and note the sequence of his moves, his releases and his spins. He wanted them to witness again what they were about to learn. (He also wanted to remind himself of his own performance because he had actually improvised much of it on the spot!)

The acrobat climbed the pole, took his position and ran through the routine again. He felt the adrenaline as the familiar fire in his chest grew and exploded outward. He couldn't help but laugh as he released the dreams he carried inside with each rush through the air.

When he returned to the eager students, he discovered that teaching could be confusing. Some immediately expressed their frustration that what he had done was not exactly what he had done the first day. Some pointed out minute differences with an edge of irritation or even disappointment.

At the same time, others joined in his adrenaline-fueled euphoria.

"Yes!" they exclaimed. "First you did that crazy spin. *How on earth* did you even think of that? Then you went right into a pivot. I never even knew you could *do that* on a trapeze!"

Those who couldn't wait to try the new and unusual moves quickly drowned out the small, disappointed group. He talked them through the mount and then had each one attempt it on their own. Some picked it up quickly while others struggled. Some even put their own unique spin on his starting sequence, thrilling him even more.

THE GROUP RESPONDS

It didn't take long for the students to point out that something wasn't quite right. Some of the things the acrobat was asking them to do contradicted what they had learned from their more experienced instructors. Basics like grip and balance were slightly different than the protocols their instructors had drilled into them. Most tried to make the changes, but the differences caused problems.

For some it was a question of retraining muscle memory. They seemed to be struggling to shift from the foundations they'd spent a lifetime learning. They would start with the things he showed them, but then quickly slip back into their old ways.

Others faced a mental block of internal resistance. They felt loyal to their original methods and told the acrobat that they were so important that they shouldn't be changed. It just *felt* wrong. One even said she felt it was a betrayal of the troupe's ancient ways to grip the bar differently, or to shift their center of gravity. The acrobat found that if he told students like her to let go of the old and embrace the new, they were prone to resist him as a teacher and even drop out of the process. He was up against an embedded *culture*.

Over the coming days, the acrobat took a deep breath and slowed down his teaching approach. He found that gently questioning the old ways allowed his students to let go a little bit at a time. Joining them on their journey of discovery kept his students from resisting him as a teacher. The questions seemed to allow them to slowly release old thoughts instead of immediately triggering their defenses.

"Look at your hands on the bar," he said. "What advantage does that grip give you when your body weight is entirely supported by your arms?"

He listened attentively to their answers before posing another question.

"Can you think of any disadvantages resulting from that grip?"

Now his students didn't just listen to him. They analyzed and thought through the processes on their own—making them much more willing to embrace their own discoveries.

YOU CAN'T DO IT THAT WAY!

As the weeks went on, word of the new training got back to the other instructors. Some listened and even dropped in to watch, excited to see some of the troupe learn new skills and new ways.

The acrobat grew aware that some of the other instructors had become concerned. Whether they had attended a training session or not, they were clearly upset that the acrobat had told the others to alter the fundamentals.

Those other instructors, especially those who had been around the longest, almost succeeded in shutting the acrobat's training down. It was only because some of the instructors were excited about the sessions (or their kids were!) that the acrobat was allowed to continue.

Several tried to discourage the acrobat by warning him about the errors of his methods and the pitfalls of abandoning the "oh-so-important" fundamentals. He might have given up if he had not received equally overt support from other leaders.

In his heart, he knew that he was different. Some were excited by "different;" others were afraid of it.

The acrobat did notice that as time went on, he lost a few students. Interestingly though, new ones regularly arrived. They spent their time working through the elements of the routine one step at a time. But something still didn't feel right. He couldn't quite figure out what it was, but he trusted it would come to him soon enough.

UN-TEACHING TO TEACH

As the days turned into weeks, the acrobat discovered that he spent almost as much time *un*-teaching his group as he did teaching. Every time one of his students was unable to complete the skills or tricks he showed them, he could trace it back to something else they had learned. Sometimes old thinking stood in the way of the student embracing new skills.

Un-teaching seemed harder than teaching. However, without it, much of the new teaching wouldn't stick, and in some cases, the new skills couldn't co-exist at all with the troupe's protocols.

Part of the difficulty of un-teaching was not changing the physical skill. It was changing the mind. The students' minds seemed a more formidable foe and a more important ally than the students' bodies. In most cases, once their minds released their old learning, the new skills came quite naturally.

> **"SOMETIMES OLD THINKING STOOD IN THE WAY OF THE STUDENT EMBRACING NEW SKILLS."**

To combat this challenge, occasionally the acrobat would take his students to places other than the practice arena. Using tree branches and vines instead of a high bar and ropes allowed his students to break a deeply conditioned train of thought.

The teaching sessions continued and one release at a time, one twist at a time, the young acrobats began to more easily run through the skills they had seen performed. Strangely, as they did, they seemed less and less excited by the new skills. Something *still* wasn't right.

He watched his students everyday as they showed up at the practice tent. Two different groups emerged from the eager students. One group began their sessions by running through each detail of what they had learned. They performed point by point what they had seen him do that first day on the trapeze.

The other group also showed up and began to warm up, but their approach was different. They had made the changes in grip and balance. They had learned all the moves. This group, however, ran through some of the tricks they had learned, but they took it a step further. They began to experiment with new movements.

Once again, the acrobat discovered that no two people saw the same things or learned in the same way. Some wanted to mimic what they had seen. Others wanted to experiment with new techniques.

He often had to adapt his teaching strategy to individual students' styles of learning. Clearly, no two people learned the same way.

WITNESSING FREEDOM

One day the acrobat walked into the practice tent and saw two young female students on the equipment, laughing and experimenting with new ideas. The look on their faces was familiar to him. The joy and laughter of their experimentation seemed almost explosive.

Then one of them got on the trapeze and began a freestyle routine. The acrobat and the young woman's friend watched in amazement. The young woman in front of them was grinning and laughing and doing things that neither one of them had ever imagined before.

When the young woman dismounted, both the acrobat and her friend ran over, unable to contain themselves, and began talking about what they had seen.

"How did you come up with *that?*"

"What was that thing you did right after the double flip?"

Their excitement was reminiscent of that first day when the acrobat had performed. They were amazed and excited by what they had seen.

"Can you teach me to do that?" the acrobat asked her.

They spent a few hours working on the routine she had created that day. It was such an exhilarating time and filled with so much life and excitement. They wrapped up the day exhausted, and the acrobat began the trek back to his own tent thinking about what had happened. His own willingness to learn and the joy he experienced as a result of it renewed his eagerness to keep teaching the others.

I think I know what it felt like for all those other young acrobats that first day, he thought. He considered what he had felt as he had watched that young woman perform a routine unlike anything he had ever dremed. In a split second, her face flashed through his mind, and he realized what he had missed in earlier training sessions.

He recalled the sheer joy on her face as she had sailed through the air. He knew that feeling well, and he saw that feeling occasionally on the faces of the young men and women who had come to learn from him. He tried to think what that feeling might be.

Happiness? he pondered.

Happiness seemed too generic. It was far more than just happiness.

Joy?

Joy is closer, he thought.

Then different words came to his mind. He flashed back to the days he had lived earthbound. He remembered the feeling of being constrained by gravity and even being constrained by the picture of himself that he had carried. He remembered in particular how desperately he ached for something he couldn't even define. It was more than simply a desire to climb and swing. It was more than simply a desire for excitement.

Something or someone had felt trapped inside of him his entire life. The feeling of being trapped and not even knowing that he was trapped had been with him until the first day he played on the trapeze without fear or insecurity. On that day, the person inside of him had been turned loose for the first time.

That was the look he had seen on the young woman's face. The feeling was more than joy. It was *release!* The feeling he saw that day as she unleashed what was inside her was freedom! In that moment he knew what had bothered him about the way he was teaching.

When the students had gathered and asked him to teach them what they had seen that day on the trapeze, he had misunderstood. While they had seen him perform a series of tricks and moves, they had seen something more. They had seen someone, for the first time ever, *fully free*—right before their eyes.

More than any performance, they had witnessed *freedom*. And while it happened on the trapeze, the freedom had less to do with the equipment and more to do with the acrobat's own discovery and self-expression. That was what the students had asked him to teach them, and yet, none of them had realized it. They hadn't even known that's what they had wanted.

A NEW PERSPECTIVE

The acrobat returned to the teaching time that next week with a new perspective but unsure how to proceed. He began, once again, by gathering them together.

"I realized something this week," he began, "I have not taught you what you asked me for."

The group responded in a variety of ways. Some wanted to reassure him that they were perfectly happy with his methods. Others were curious and waited to hear more.

"What you saw happen that day on the trapeze was far more than a set of acrobatic moves. Remember, while you were all here learning and practicing to be acrobats, I was living on a farm, learning to work the ground. I had it drilled into me that my place in the world was to plow and plant. The whole time something inside of me fought back against that life."

The students listened intently. He had told them before how he had missed all those years, but they likely had never considered what his life had been like outside their troupe. Strangely, as he described the feeling of being trapped inside himself, many of them nodded, clearly familiar with that feeling.

"When I first came back to you, my family, I thought I would immediately take to the life and practices that were so familiar to you, but it wasn't that easy. I had some unlearning to do. I had to completely change the way I saw myself. Some of you may remember I had physical challenges to overcome. But that day you saw me on the trapeze for the first time, you saw more than a routine, you saw me *unleashed*.

"When you asked me to teach you, I think we all thought that what I should teach you was the routine I had performed and maybe that is all that you wanted. But what you saw that day was something we all need and crave. We all hunger to be *turned loose*. To be *free*.

> "WE ALL HUNGER TO BE TURNED LOOSE. TO BE FREE"

"We all had some unlearning to do when I began to teach you the moves. It was foreign, and on some days, it felt like we might be doing something wrong. But what I now know is that the *un*learning opens the door for what you truly want. Once you unlearn what you have been told, you must find out what is inside of you, and then each of you can be released. Each of you can be set free.

"Here is what I now understand. You spent years learning physical skills under the direction of your trainers. You needed that. That training gave you the strength and flexibility, the agility and confidence, to perform amazing feats. But even that direction came with limitations. The protocols you learned that gave you foundations came with limitations. None of us knew that, and no one did it on purpose. It simply limited you from certain kinds of movement and certain kinds of thinking.

"You pushed up against the limitations of those foundations and found that some of them were deeply constraining. As you let go of those constraints—as you unlearned them—you gained the ability to do the moves that I had done that first day, but those tricks could become tomorrow's constraints. If I teach you to mimic me, I simply move you from one set of constraints to another. Now that you have permission to unlearn, I must change the way I am teaching you.

"I must now help you find the moves and ideas that are buried inside you. Otherwise, a year from now you will have to unlearn all the moves that came from inside my soul. We must now change our target. Learning was a necessary step. Unlearning opened the door. But now, each of you must begin to discover what is inside you and learn to unleash that. You cannot spend the rest of your life trying to limit who you are and what's inside of you, even if that limitation comes from mimicking someone else who has found release.

"Today we are done learning my moves on the trapeze. I want you all to show me *your* moves."

With that they all gathered at the trapeze. Some had no idea what to do. Others had been working on things either in their minds or in private that they wanted to exhibit. A few others gained the freedom—the release—to try new ideas and new moves. They all stood in awe of what they saw as each person took their chance to turn loose what was inside them. It was both frightening and exhilarating.

Well, almost all stood in awe. A small handful seemed disappointed. They likely had only wanted to learn the moves they had seen that day so many weeks ago. They gradually drifted out of the practice sessions and returned to the life they had always known.

For the others, the acrobat saw that the training continued but took on a whole new direction. Not only did some of the other students take on instructional roles, relationships also changed.

Somehow as the acrobat shifted to teaching them how to discover what was inside each of them, he was drawn to know each of them better. How could he help them discover what was inside them if he did not have an idea who they were as individuals?

Knowing his students seemed to be just as important as knowing the things he taught them.

He, along with his students, also seemed to develop a much greater capacity to tolerate "mistakes." Discovering new techniques, skills and possibilities was more like a growth process than an educational process. What had previously seemed like mistakes now seemed to be a part of the learning process.

From this point on, his process was as much about helping them discover themselves as it was about passing on skills. Just as he had lived on the farm, his students had been restrained by how they saw themselves. At this level, new perspectives seemed a necessary pre-requisite to new skills.

The training classes had become a process of discovery for both students and teacher. And in this way, both teacher and student thrived like never before.

LEARNING, UNLEARNING AND UNLEASHING

As you've seen in this parable, learning the foundations is crucial. Whether it's learning the ABCs, the major scale, the periodic table, the rules of grammar or math facts, these all provide a basis for greater expression and even deeper learning. But these are not the end goal. They are merely the beginning, the support for what comes next.

And just as important as it is to learn the foundations, unlearning is equally important to truly move toward change. Unlearning allows for growth and possibilities.

"UNLEARNING ALLOWS FOR GROWTH AND POSSIBILITIES."

These processes—learning and unlearning—are still not the ultimate goal. They simply point the way. Or perhaps more accurately, they open the way, because what comes next is still learning—a new way of learning.

I share this allegory at the beginning of this book for a reason. It's more than a sweet story. It illustrates many of the points you will learn throughout this book, and hopefully, gets your mind moving, questioning how to facilitate change in others so that they can be unleashed. That's the goal. We're not superimposing our ideas or will on them. We're helping them discover their true selves.

But before we can help them do that, we have to start at the beginning and answer an all-important question: *What does it mean to learn?*

STUDY GUIDE

KEY CONCEPTS

- Some obstacles to learning are rooted in previous learning.

- Unlearning is an important part of life change.

- Questions can help you know your audience.

- The expectations of others can impede learning.

- Real life change is tied to *Identity*.

SKILL BUILDERS

1. Think about things you have learned that you have had to "un-learn." How did the process of "unlearning" occur for you?

2. Think of someone you know who seems "unleashed." What do you see or hear that gives the sense that they are "unleashed"?

3. If you are teaching others, watch this week for what you can learn from your students and make note of it in a journal.

CHAPTER 2

LEARNING ABOUT LEARNING

The most important part of teaching is to teach what it is to know.
—Simone Weil

The teacher who is indeed wise does not bid you to enter the house of his wisdom but rather leads you to the threshold of your mind.
—Khalil Gibran

How does the kid who has recently begun his study of the martial arts win a tournament defeating students with years of experience? In the first version of the classic movie *The Karate Kid,* we see young Daniel defeat his nemesis against all odds and, of course, win the heart of the girl.

The knee-jerk answer to the question is that Daniel can win because he's merely a character in a movie and not a real-life person. The second, deeper answer lies at the heart of this chapter and the foundation of this book.

Daniel had a teacher who understood that if his student was going to have any chance at all against the more experienced martial artist, he would have to *learn differently.* The way his opponents learned had taken years. Daniel did not have years. He had two months. He would have to learn in *a different way.*

Daniel was a young man from Jersey who moved into a new world. He found himself surrounded by a strange culture and shackled by his own limitations. His subsequent training at the hands of Mr. Miyagi was a great demonstration of how teaching in unexpected ways produces lasting change.

Little did Daniel realize that the first obstacle he would have to overcome was his intense desire to learn.

HE THOUGHT HE KNEW

Daniel had watched classes and had seen how the other kids learned karate. When he enlisted the help of his new teacher, he thought he knew *what* he needed to learn, and as a result, he thought he knew *how* he needed to learn.

Like Daniel, our expectations are primary filters to our own learning process…and often not in helpful ways. For Daniel to advance quickly and compete adequately, his learning had to bypass all his preconceptions. He would soon be up against young men who had years of practice, ingrained muscle memory, and mental training by another great master—time.

When the mind has built-in expectations, whether conscious or not, it automatically fills in gaps with whatever prior experience or information is available. For this reason,

> **"THE WILLINGNESS OF TEACHERS TO VIOLATE EXPECTATIONS CAN BE A TREASURED GIFT TO THEIR STUDENTS."**

preconceived ideas or expectations can be a great obstacle to deep learning. The willingness of teachers to violate expectations can be a treasured gift to their students.

Daniel didn't realize that his limitations were not simply based on what he had and had not learned. His limitations were also rooted in *the way* he had learned. Nobody had ever told him he could learn in more than one way.

So Daniel—eager, in a hurry, certain he knew what he needed, and motivated by young love—was ready to begin his classes. He was both disappointed and angry when his teacher instead stood him in front of a car giving very specific and pointed instructions about how to apply and remove the wax.

"Wax on, Wax off." became not only an iconic movie quote for years to come, but it also became embedded in moviegoers' unconscious minds as a metaphor for self-defense and blocking the attack of an enemy. For Daniel, it was embedded not only in his unconscious, but it was also forever embedded in his physiology and muscle memory. It sneaked past his expectations and became a part of him from that moment forward.

The beauty is that, even while the young man expressed frustration and resisted his training, he was learning far more than he realized. He wasn't simply learning defense; he was learning about himself. *He was learning about learning.*

Mr. Miyagi understood this. He knew Daniel needed more than skills to practice. He needed something deeper to change.

A skilled teacher believes the *way* you know something matters more than *what* you know.

You read a survival book differently in your living room than you do stranded in the middle of the rainforest. How you understand the Bible depends on what you believe about it and what your motive is for reading it. Do you read the Bible in order to win arguments and be right? Do you read it for instructions about right and wrong living? Or do you read it because it is a conduit for the voice of Someone you love…Someone who cares for you?

YOU CAN KNOW

Jesus told His students, "…you shall know the truth, and the truth shall make you free." This is one of the most powerful and well-known statements in the Gospels. However, one of the biggest barriers to becoming free is revealed by Jesus in that single sentence. He says you must *know* the truth.

In *The Karate Kid,* Daniel was completely unaware that his style of learning was incompatible with what he needed. Similarly, we may be unaware that our understanding of how to "know the truth" is incompatible with the kind of truth that transforms people and sets them free.

In the same way that Daniel had expectations of what and how he needed to learn, we have expectations of what it means "to know" the truth—or anything else. If knowing the truth is the pathway to freedom, we will, of course, set out on a pathway to knowing, but that can be a useless pursuit if we never consider that "knowing" can have multiple meanings and multiple pathways. We assume that we must learn the same way we have always learned. And if we teach, we assume that we must teach the same way that we were always taught.

Big mistake.

Let me explain.

Years ago, I had an opportunity to speak to a church on Sunday morning. It was my first opportunity to speak in that setting, and the pastor was a friend of mine. As we discussed preparations for the upcoming services, he suggested that I create handouts ahead of time. He had a method that included providing service notes with a single word blank in each point's sentence. His congregation would listen and "fill in the blank" when he covered it. He suggested I follow suit.

Respectfully, I had to ask: "So…is this required, or are you simply providing an option I can use?"

He responded with a statement about learning theory. It had something to do with how much more people "learn" when they engage in the process.

I smiled and said, "So here's the thing: I don't want people to learn this morning."

His brow furrowed. "What? Why wouldn't you want people to learn?"

I chuckled. "I guess I *do* want them to *learn*," I replied. "Except I want them to learn to think for themselves, rather than learn to mimic what *I* think."

My friend still had questions in his eyes. I was hoping he would see that I was pointing out the difference between teaching others what I thought versus having them take the material and synthesize it for themselves.

HOW DO YOU SEE?

We all wear lenses that we have looked through for a lifetime, but often, we have not looked *at* them. What filters have we been looking through? The most basic of all these lenses is our understanding of what it means "to know" something. How people come to know as well as what "knowing" actually means should be the first two questions posed by every communicator—from parent to president.

> "WE ALL WEAR LENSES THAT WE HAVE LOOKED THROUGH FOR A LIFETIME, BUT OFTEN, WE HAVE NOT LOOKED AT THEM."

Consider how widely varied it can be to "know" something. There's a big difference between the kind of knowing that public school teachers advocate for test-taking and the kind of knowing that took place between Adam and Eve resulting in the conception of a child.

When teachers say they want you to know certain items for a test, they are simply saying they want you to commit those items to memory for the purpose of recall and recitation. In this case, the word "know" means "memorize and recall."

When the Bible says, "Adam knew Eve" and she conceived a child, we see a very different meaning. Adam, who had once carried Eve in his rib and who now walked with her and beside her, knew her one way as separate beings. When they knew each other again in deep union, the result was new life. In this case, the word "know" means "encounter and engage deeply with an open heart, mind and body, restoring the once familiar and always intended connection between each other."

These two very different, yet completely accurate, meanings for the word "know" demonstrate that the word "know" can have multiple meanings.

"Knowing" is a complex idea and yet it is one we participate in daily. We want to know:

- What time is dinner?

- Who is your 3:00 appointment?

- What is that person's phone number?

These are only a few of the ways we "know" our way through every given day. The beauty of these "*knowings*" is that they are all basic facts. Time, name, numbers—they are all data that we can store and recall.

But consider the question: "Do you *know* what I mean?" Now we begin to approach the slippery slope of the various ways people know. We see this phenomenon when a husband and wife both say they "know" a certain person, but then have polarizing opinions of that person. We see it when someone asks if you know music or art, or even a specific work of art.

These kinds of abstract "*knowings*" exhibit just how many ways there are "to know"—so much more than just those mentioned regarding school teachers and Adam and Eve. There is a wide scale of what it means to know something, and our communication often slides around that scale haphazardly.

As a communicator who looks to help people change their lives, I want to understand exactly what manner of "knowing" will make the greatest impact possible on my hearers. For instance, does "knowing" to them mean...

- To memorize (for example, knowing the dates for a history test),

- To become familiar with (for example, knowing a song, or a friend),

- To grasp frameworks (for example, to know music), or

- To experience (for example, to know how delicious a chocolate cake is)?

If I hit the center of the target for one form of "knowing" and it is not the form of "knowing" that will bring the greatest lasting change, I might have the misperception that I have accomplished my goal.

Worse, I can begin to criticize my listeners if they misunderstand me or remain unchanged. Unconsciously, I may begin to project the reasons for the misunderstanding onto them rather than examine my own strategy.

THE WAY YOU KNOW MATTERS

As we continue this conversation about "ways of knowing," it is important to reiterate that the way you come to *know* something is deeply connected to how you know that something.

Sadly, in our culture, we are seldom taught how to learn. Because we are taught by specific, Western educational processes, we unconsciously assume that these processes define what it means "to learn." Daniel's teacher had a different cultural point-of-view about learning; thus, his approach to helping Daniel learn was vastly different and unexpected.

Learning has many rich and nuanced processes. To simplify it down to memorizing and repeating data often invalidates the amazing capacity of the human mind to synthesize and improvise as well as create wonder and beauty.

As we discover what it means to learn, the mysteries of the cosmos open. Some of those wonders are simply waiting to be revealed. Thought processes are something we use every day, but we seldom, if ever, consider or discuss them.

If we never take the time to examine the various influences our own mind and soul have on our thinking and knowing, then we always take in new information on a single channel. We never consider that other channels exist. Here are a few channels we use to take in information…

- Intuition: *What kind of person is he/she?*

- Experience: *What kind of bike trail is that?*

- Spiritual: *What was that shift in the room?*

- Observation and Senses: *What kind of dog is that?*

We have all attended school in some form, and many of us have attended some form of Western education. While we dutifully attended classes and completed our assignments, the majority of us never questioned the way we were taught. We naturally assumed that the way we were taught is the way teaching should occur.

> **"THE WAY WE KNOW THINGS MATTERS MORE THAN WHAT WE KNOW."**

The result? We developed a way of learning that we seldom question.

Thought process then has far less to do with *what* we know and far more to do with the *way* we know. It has to do with the way we learn, how we take in information, and most importantly what we do with information as it comes in.

Thought processes are patterns in the mind that tell incoming information what to do. If you usually worry, all information is told to feed your worry. If you are usually optimistic, all information is told to feed your optimism.

SAYING TWO THINGS AT ONCE

People attend our *Think Differently Learn Differently* workshop to become better communicators. Our workshop is about helping think about communication in new ways.

Once we've spent time establishing some rapport, I begin with this thought: "For the next two days, I will always be saying two things at once. If you only pay attention to what I say, you will only learn half of what you are here to learn."

After a pause, I continue.

"The *way* we know things matters more than *what* we know. Our most potent messages are the unseen ones. Be sure to *listen* to what I say, but also be sure to notice *the way* I say things. Both are important, and both are part of our time together."

I want the attendees to understand that communication is more than words. Whether you and those you communicate with notice it or not, both of your messages—1) what you say and 2) how you say it—are sent and received. As a speaker, teacher, or influencer, this is your potential superpower.

Every message has a method, or a *way*, in which the message is sent. The most powerful communication happens when the method and the message *match*. The method, or the *way*, is often the least attended to, and yet it is always the more powerful of the two.

When the method and the message are incongruent, the method takes precedence and becomes the message. So, when the words do not line up with the delivery, the delivery not only negates the words, it sends a message of its own. Marriage therapists spend much of their time helping clients understand this truth. Let's look at an illustration that demonstrates how the method can become the message:

> *He sits in the room not far from her, but his mind is in another place altogether. Whether his thoughts are on his work or his hobby, he is in the room but not with her. And she knows it.*

> *She asks the question. "Honey, how do you feel about me?"*

> *He doesn't look up. He is vaguely aware that she has spoken, but her words don't quite get through the fog of his own thoughts. "What?" he mutters, still only half present.*

So far, the husband's method takes precedence. The way he communicates is itself a message. He sends a message about his connection to his wife, and it is the reason she asked the question. In his disconnection, he doesn't pick up on the shift in the atmosphere. She is fearful, but it shows itself as anger.

> *"I said," she reiterates, her voice now a bit icy, "how do you feel about me?"*

The wife's method, or her way of communicating, is a message now too. She wants him to turn and attend to her. She has not said it with words, but her method has stepped up the intensity.

The husband's method (disconnection) is as loud as the wife's method (increased frustration), but it trumps her method because it is disengaged. He hears her message but not her method, and he responds to her words but not to her fear.

> *"I love you," he mumbles half-heartedly, knowing this is "the right answer."*

What do you hear in the dialogue? How do you interpret the words of both people? Do you recognize any possible biases or, at least, prior experiences you bring to your hearing?

The husband's method and message are incongruent. Half-hearted mumbling from a place of disconnection is entirely out-of-sync with the reality behind the words, "I love you." And in a split second, the incongruence thrusts his method in the face of his loved one. The method becomes the message, and conflict ensues.

Now imagine if this scene had unfolded differently…

> "Honey," she ventures, "how do you feel about me?"
>
> He sets his phone down and turns toward her, making eye contact. His eyes search hers for the rest of the question. He hears the words but assumes the words must have come from somewhere beyond mild curiosity.
>
> "How do I feel about you?" He leans in and puts a hand on her arm. He sees fear, or at least insecurity. "You are the rarest of women. How did I get to be the one to answer this question?"
>
> She warms to him, and her fear begins to subside. Her smile feels like relief.
>
> "I feel lucky is how I feel," he continues, "lucky to have found you and lucky that you responded when I dared to ask you out. I feel fortunate that I have the chance to discover new facets of you every day, and to see again things I've seen many times before. How do I feel? I am crazy about you."
>
> She leans on his shoulder and presses into him. His words found her. She feels at home.

The wife's question had meaning beyond the obvious. In the second example, the husband was aware enough to not only speak but to *listen* with his eyes. His method matched his message, and his words reached from his soul to hers. Whether or not he knew he was saying two things at once, his method and his message were exactly the same.

The more we can purposefully match our method to our message, the more powerful our communication becomes.

Communicators in every setting are subject to this dynamic. From parent to child, from pastor to congregation, from teacher to student, and from boss to subordinate we send at least two messages every time we speak. Our intentionality about that can multiply the impact of every exchange.

Mr. Miyagi taught his student some of his most important lessons without a word. He taught him about trust by having him do the unexpected. He taught him to settle his soul by not responding to his urgency. He taught him to think in a new way by teaching him in an unexpected way. His most important lessons and the ones that pierced most deeply were the ones that were taught without language. They were taught implicitly, or covertly.

> **"THE MORE WE CAN PURPOSEFULLY MATCH OUR METHOD TO OUR MESSAGE, THE MORE POWERFUL OUR COMMUNICATION BECOMES."**

I remember once hearing a man with a Bible teach about joy. With a sour face and an edge of anger, he spoke for almost an hour accurately and intelligently about what the Bible says about joy.

Like Daniel, I learned a lot that day...none of which had to do with joy. Like Daniel, the deepest lessons I learned that day were the ones that were taught implicitly. I learned about the value (or danger) of separating your thoughts from your heart. I learned that this man valued intellect more than congruence. I learned that you can teach ideas from the Bible separate from the heart of its Author. And I learned the importance of tending to both what I say and the way I say it.

COVERT AND OVERT COMMUNICATION

The reason we are always saying two things at once is because communication always contains two types of messages. Every exchange contains an overt message, the information being broadcast, and various covert messages, the non-verbal implications.

Covert messages like eye contact, tone, context, and various other external factors, always accompany the overt. This is simply another way to describe the idea of message (overt) and method (covert). Covert messages are neither good nor bad, they are simply messages. Healthy and effective communication takes place when the covert messages are in agreement with the overt messages.

IF

OVERT
(SPOKEN COMMUNICATION / INFORMATION)

MATCHES

COVERT
(NON-VERBAL COMMUNICATION / RELATIONSHIP)

THEN

COMMUNICATION IS HEALTHY AND EFFECTIVE

Overt communication is always about the transfer of information or data. Covert communication is almost always about relationship. It is at this covert level that we convey value or disdain, kindness, or apathy. It is at this unspoken level that we communicate what others mean to us and even what the process of communicating means to us.

While some people are more attuned to the covert level of communication, everyone receives at this level. When our method is congruent with our message, the message is exponentially more powerful. When our method is congruent with our message, the power of truth can pierce the hearts of our listeners and transform the way they both see and experience themselves and the world around them. Congruence in our communication makes our message less about words and more about power—that is, power to bring deep and lasting change.

When we purposefully align our method and message with the Breath of God, our communication can help people become the men or women they were created to be.

Now that we better understand how people learn and how covert and overt communication go together, let's dive into how we can invoke positive change in our listeners by looking at the words, ideas, and structures that form the way we learn.

STUDY GUIDE

KEY CONCEPTS

- The *way* you learn affects the *way* you know.

- The *way* you know affects the impact of the content (knowledge).

- Expectations of how we should learn can prevent new ways of learning.

- Every expressed message has two levels: the Overt and the Covert.

- The Overt level carries the information. The Covert level shows the relationship.

SKILL BUILDERS

1. Ask yourself these questions:

   - What does it mean to know a song?

   - What does it mean to know your friend?

   - What does it mean to know right from wrong?

   - What does it mean to know the answer to a test?

   - What does it mean to know pain and sorrow?

   - What does it mean to know you are fully accepted?

   - What does it mean to know how cold or hot it is outside?

2. This week as you have a conversation or watch a speaker, watch for both Overt and Covert communication. Ask yourself, "What is being communicated at each level?"

3. Think about your closest relationships. Do your covert messages align with the words you are saying?

4. Consider who the most impactful teacher was in your life. What was it about them that impacted you?

5. This week, try to speak to those you love and intentionally use fewer words. How does that affect your communication?

CHAPTER 3

INVOKING CHANGE: IT STARTS WITH WORDS, IDEAS, AND STRUCTURES

"As social creatures, we are our stories and definitions and we are obliged to keep them in good working order."
—Efan, Luken, and Luken

"EEEEE eeeeee EEEE eee EEEEE!"
—Flipper

Jane was on her third marriage and this one was not going well. She didn't blame the men in her past. She knew she had hurt them deeply and she felt sure that—in their shoes—she wouldn't have stayed married to her either. She blamed herself because *she knew better*. She had grown up in a normal home with a normal family, or so she had told herself. She had even grown up in church.

Yet, despite all those advantages, she still yearned for the attention of men in unhealthy ways. Their attention was like oxygen to her. She didn't want to crave it, but without it, she seemed unable to breathe. Her compulsion had fueled a cycle of inappropriate relationships, regardless of her marital status. She had tried to change but often found herself inhaling this destructive cycle.

She had read books and listened to speakers, but still struggled to control her self-destructive habits. Everything she read and heard only served to make her feel worse about her inability to stop hurting people.

Why was it that everything she learned didn't help her?

Jane isn't the only person with a lifetime of battles like this. As far back as history records, men and women alike have always faced similar struggles. Why is it that we are unable to

> **"WORDS, IDEAS, AND STRUCTURES ARE THE BUILDING BLOCKS OF MEANINGFUL COMMUNICATION."**

change our most destructive behaviors or thoughts? Why is it that even when we know better, we still repeatedly fall into trouble? Why is it that even when we learn ways to change, our "learnings" may make no difference, or at times, they even make our struggle worse?

It is these questions, and more importantly, the quest to find meaningful answers to them, that has driven my life and work for the last three decades. In this chapter, we will look at the reason why change is often elusive.

Every conversation about change begins with the same building block: language. But while language may increase our awareness of a need to change, it often falls short of providing the mechanisms. Change takes place at a much deeper level. We must understand that:

WE COMMUNICATE WITH WORDS,

WE CONCEPTUALIZE IN IDEAS,

BUT

WE GROW AND CHANGE AT THE LEVEL OF STRUCTURE

Words, ideas, and structures are the building blocks of meaningful communication. We'll look at each of these in this chapter. In order to produce beautiful music it is important to first learn our notes and scales. Similarly, before we set out to produce meaningful change in the lives of others we need to understand the building blocks of communication.

WE COMMUNICATE WITH WORDS

Words are a basic unit of communication. Giving thought to their limitations and power allows us to wield them with maximum impact. This may seem obvious, but this is more than a simple point.

Words have power, but only as symbols. When we utter the word "car," an automobile does not materialize in our mouths. A word represents something, and that representation attaches to meaning in the mind of every listener (or reader). Ironically, a single word might mean something entirely different in the mind of every single person who hears it.

I often help couples recognize that symbols, or words, do not have the same meaning to each of them. When talking about money, they must understand that money, while possessing concrete and measurable *amounts,* can have abstract and varied *meanings.*

To one partner, money may represent security. If this is the case, the most important way this individual can use money is to save it. Spending represents a loss of security and triggers a strong emotional response.

To another partner, money may represent love or affection. To this person, the most important use of money is to give it in the form of gifts or experiences. Spending money fosters a deep emotional response because it is an expression of value and care.

If these two people are in relationship and talk about money, they may believe that they are having the same conversation, but they're not. The failure to recognize that money is a symbol and that both have different attachments to that symbol sets up conflict. If they never move from words to ideas, they will wonder why they struggle to solve financial problems.

Interestingly, their conflict has more to do with words and ideas than it does with actual dollars. If they talk about spending, one feels relief while the other feels pressure. If they talk about saving, the other feels relief while the one feels unloved. Because of the various meanings, words can result in confusion.

People lose connection with one another regularly over words. The word "Christian" in one culture can reference a persecuting army, while in another culture the word can reference the martyred minority. Therefore, it is important to learn the symbols of the people we address. While a word may carry a great weight and specific meaning to you, tune in to your listeners and consider that words that feel soothing to you might stir anxiety in others.

As a speaker and teacher, use the words that communicate best to your audience. Recognize that even though your audience might speak English, their use of certain terms and phrases might differ from your own. Do not make words a graven image that refuses to change.

Jane, who we met earlier, had likely heard a lot of words about change. She had read books and listened to speakers talk about change. But since words alone are merely symbols, they could have triggered a sense of shame or other emotional response. Words like "should" or "push through" can elicit an emotional state that might

> **"THE GREATER THE DISTANCE BETWEEN THE WORD AND THE MEANING IN THE HEART OF THE SPEAKER, THE LESS POWER A WORD HAS."**

increase her struggle rather than decrease it. Or she might have heard the same words for so long that they had lost their meaning.

Words alone, without the power to instigate change, can be more than just lifeless. They can be devastating.

WORDS HAVE A SHELF LIFE

It is important to remember that words are not only symbols, but also that the meaning attached to them can grow, shift and age. The phrase "I love you" first uttered by young lovers is laden with excitement and fear. Years later the same three words can come to mean "see you after work."

When we first have an idea or an experience, we generate words from the newness of the experience. Over time the repetition of those words lose their meaning or potency. Rather than coming from fresh experience, they begin to be recited from memory.

In the re-telling of a story or description, the symbol and the meaning begin to drift apart. The words no longer carry the weight that they did with their first utterance. The greater the distance between the word and the meaning in the heart of the speaker, the less power a word has.

From one generation to next, a similar disconnect happens. Words that describe the experience of one generation are used to describe the fables of the next. The generation after that uses the same words to describe a memory. The exact same word moves from something concrete and meaningful to a vague idea.

We see this decay when we consider Bible translations from various eras. Consider the King James translation that regularly uses words like "thee" and "thou." While we can recognize the antiquity of these word forms and translate them into modern pronouns, words like "lasciviousness" become trickier. Or consider the depth of meaning that is lost when passages like 1 Corinthians 1:30 are paraphrased or modernized: "But of him are ye in Christ Jesus, who of God is made unto us wisdom, and righteousness, and sanctification, and redemption."

While the words are accurate, they are also antiquated and do not carry with them the quivering excitement and immediate experience of profound change. The shelf life of these words can rob them of the power contained in the ideas they are meant to communicate.

WE CONCEPTUALIZE IN IDEAS

While words are symbols, the meanings *attached* to our words are ideas. Ideas are concepts or groups of concepts expressed by a range of words. They could be abstract ideas like "life," "liberty," or "happiness" or they could be more concrete ideas like a "house" or a "car." Regardless, ideas are bigger in our mind than words. They are the vocabulary of an active mind. These clusters of concepts fill our mind and can be described, synthesized, refined and/or expressed.

An idea is relatively easy to change as it is often in flux anyway. New and improved ideas are the ongoing process of a developing mind. Much like a set of LEGO® bricks, ideas can be combined, deconstructed, or completely wiped out. They are what we pass on when we communicate, give advice, or provide steps to overcome something. We package and bundle ideas together in sentences made up of words.

Consider again Jane who opened this chapter. She had heard a *lot* of ideas. The clusters of words she heard gave her the ideas of the speakers or writers she had pursued. She heard ideas about right and wrong. She read ideas about strategies to manage her behavior. She even concocted ideas about how she might stay completely away from even the possibility of engaging in destructive relationships. Many of these ideas stirred up the hope of change, but like the words that had no power, the ideas alone always disappointed. What was it going to take for her to finally change?

In many cases, those ideas had worked for one author or even a group of people. At times, they even provided Jane with temporary change and a sense of hope.

The proposal of a new idea is a common strategy for the self-help or spiritual growth movements. Try this. Do that. Implement these steps or methods. Good ideas help people, but not all ideas help all people because all people are different.

Unless an idea deconstructs and reconstructs the pictures or images that people have inside their minds, deep and lasting change will not happen. Inside our souls, we have all built an internal representation of our external world. People live, grow, and change based on these representations, or *structures*, that their minds have built.

WE GROW AND CHANGE AT THE LEVEL OF STRUCTURE

The idea of structure goes by several labels but by using the label "structure," I hope to keep you from falling into the trap of familiarity or of making assumptions that could rob you of the richness of discovery. Let me illustrate.

My wife and I took a wildlife cruise off the coast of San Diego, hoping to see any one of a variety of whales. We did not see whales that day, but we did see a huge pod of about 300-400 dolphins. They surrounded us. They leapt out of the water around us and rode the bow-wave of our small craft. They put on a delightful show and seemed somehow to engage with our boatful of humans.

Our captain explained how dolphins navigate effectively through the waters. They and other sonar-guided mammals create an image of their external world inside their skulls. The sound waves emitted are bounced back from the surrounding physical world. Those sound waves then develop a 3-D "map" inside the dolphins' brains.

Like a virtual reality game, dolphins interact with that internal map as if it is reality itself. This is a structure. That structure, or 3-D map, inside the dolphins' minds provides all the important information dolphins need to navigate safely and effectively in their watery world. They navigate the structure inside their heads, but the map so accurately represents the outside world, they can swim with speed and precision in difficult undersea terrain.

That map in their heads helps them know when they are safe and when they are in danger. It tells them when obstacles are ahead and when their way is free of barriers. All of their decisions and actions come from reading that internal map. They live their entire lives interacting with that internal structure—and so do we.

The greatest difference is that our structures are not constructed by sound waves, rather they are constructed by our senses and our emotional and cognitive interpretations. Because of this, they are not nearly as accurate as the structures that guide dolphins. Our structures are constructed through a lifetime of experiences. We send our senses out and our best understanding of what bounces back becomes the building material for our internal representations.

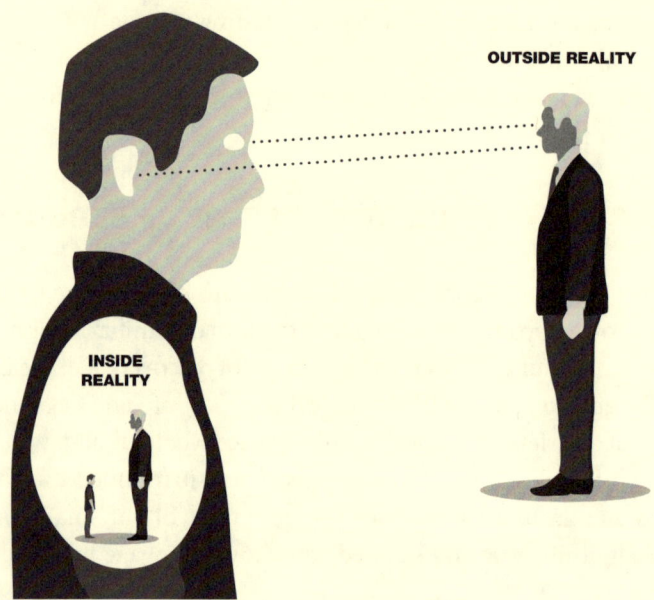

Interestingly, our best understanding arrives in the years where we understand the least. Our childhood interpretations become our adult realities. So it is that we build these structures early in life, and, as we do, the structures become not only a guide, but also a filter through which every other image of the world must pass.

It is for this reason that we read in the Talmud, "We do not see the world as it is, we see it as we are." We see the world through structures and filters comprised of our historical experiences.

Because we navigate by structure, words and ideas alone cannot bring meaningful change. Meaningful change must take place at the structural level. We act, think, feel, and relate based on the structures we have built over our lifetime.

- Our structures are like filters that only allow in what already "fits."

- Our structures are like frameworks, sculpting all input into pre-existing shapes.

- Our structures are like colored lenses, distorting all input to fit only the colors we already know.

- Our structures are like censors that delete any information that doesn't already have an internal category.

We all have internal representations of our external world, and we all have a way that we construct these representations. Once built, these structures reinforce their own existence and stability. Words and ideas come in through our senses and mind and arrange themselves around these structures that are so firmly entrenched in our souls. Even the best ideas are adapted and integrated.

Right now as you read this, all of your structures are being challenged in the exact same way the acrobat was challenged to think differently about teaching his students. Remember when he felt something wasn't quite right but couldn't put words to that feeling? Change often starts before understanding crystallizes. Relax and trust the process!

Meaningful change comes when the structures we have built are called into question, and we begin to understand and utilize a new way. We begin to tear down and rebuild these structures as we begin to see things in a different way.

> "THE GAP BETWEEN OUR INTERNAL REPRESENTATION AND OUR EXTERNAL REALITY IS THE DISTANCE WE MUST TRAVEL TO FIND TRUE FREEDOM."

Now, let's look at the source and process of how we create these structures. By learning their origins, we can also learn to deconstruct them—and bring lasting change to those we want to reach.

55

INTERNAL REPRESENTATIONS

Structures are the ways that we internally represent the external world. They are how we experience life—our perceptions, emotions, and thought processes. They dictate what we accept as "real." They are internal representations of our external reality...and they are distorted by our filters. The gap between our internal representation and our external reality is the distance we must travel to find true freedom.

Remember Jane? Her self destructive behavior grew not only from bad thinking but also from an internal picture of herself and others. These pictures had been built over the course of her life.

She had an internal picture, or structure, of herself. She had an internal picture, or structure, of men. And she had an internal picture, or structure, of God. Structures go by many names, but regardless of what they are called, it is more important to understand how they function.

Jane tried to learn her way to freedom. She read words and listened to ideas that entered her senses and then entered her mind. Once those building blocks entered her mind, however, they encountered Jane's structures. Those words and ideas had to either find a way to fit what already existed in her structures, or they simply would not stick.

Structures function to analyze and organize incoming data. Like a filter, they allow certain things to come in and prevent other things from getting through. Not only will they allow certain ideas to enter, but they will also tell those ideas where they should be categorized.

When data gets through in the form of words or experience, it is categorized as an exception or a rule, as a fact or an opinion, as true or false. Of course, none of those categories necessarily depend on reality. Instead, they depend entirely on what the pre-existing structure perceives to be reality.

Our structures are like virtual reality maps. They are built on imperfect perceptions, yet we interact with them as if they are reality. Can you see why changing the structures of your listeners is a crucial element of effective communication? If you change or even modify one of your listener's structures, you change the way they view and interact with reality from that point on.

Would it surprise you to know that when Jesus said, "You will know the truth and the truth will make you free," the Greek word for truth can be translated "reality?"

PARADIGMS, ARCHETYPES, AND INTROJECTS

Three commonly understood structures are paradigms, archetypes, and introjects. Each of these structures has a slightly different function while providing the same level of organizing, filtering, and censoring for incoming data.

Often these structures are obstacles to change. Learning how to reach through filters and connect to structures is paramount to reaching an audience. By understanding what these structures are and how they function, we can help them become great allies, rather than obstacles, in the quest for change.

PARADIGMS

A paradigm is like an internal roadmap of reality, or how the world "is" to an individual. Big ideas like "what is right" and "how things should work" are paradigms. Like dolphins, everyone swims full speed in these structures as if they *are* reality...until the paradigm begins to collapse.

Loss and other painful or shocking circumstances can bring a paradigm crashing down. Lesser experiences are simply assimilated by the roadmap and explained away by pre-existing beliefs. Someone else's loss can be understood by a simplistic paradigm. However, when an individual suffers a personal loss, it can be a shock to that system of beliefs and forces a re-examination of that belief. For instance, if a friend's spouse is losing a fight to cancer, we may simplistically explain it away as, "She doesn't have enough faith." But if *our* spouse gets cancer and nothing seems to work, we may find ourselves questioning our paradigm about what faith is and how it works altogether.

What if we, as instigators of change, could communicate in such a way that we invited the same questioning *without* a crisis? What if it were possible, through understanding the territory and the tools, to begin chipping away at these paradigms and cause people to question the harmful beliefs they have sculpted?

Could someone like our friend Jane, who had listened to teachers but was unable to change, begin to question the core beliefs that had locked her into her destructive cycle?

Jane had a paradigm, an internal picture, about her value. In a family and a culture that had rewarded her with connection and acceptance based on her sexuality, she had quickly assimilated a seemingly immovable paradigm. Her value was intertwined with her sexuality.

That structure alone provided a powerful sense of loss when she was not engaged in attention-seeking behavior with men. She also gained a sense of power, value, and identity when she could get a man to turn his attention toward her. Jane's paradigm was the overarching roadmap that dictated her experience regardless of what words or ideas she heard.

ARCHETYPES

While paradigms are roadmaps of reality, archetypes are big constructs about concepts—things like good and evil and justice and love. Everyone has archetypal structures about these big ideas. We often assign these concepts to characters, like the archetype of forbidden, tragic love we find in *Romeo and Juliet*. They are often shaped early in life.

Classes on ethics and moral issues may invite an examination of these internal definitions, but once archetypal structures are formed, they are usually only changed by crisis or by a skilled communicator with the wisdom and patience to chip away at these monolithic ideas.

Jane had a picture of "love" anchored on the inside of her soul. To her, love was a powerful atmosphere that, if she could breathe it in, she would not only survive, but she would also finally be somebody.

Her picture of "love" and "self" were completely woven together with sex and masculine attention. This guiding structure—this archetype—was not a construct of conscious thought. It was a bedrock of her understanding of love before she could ever speak. Her early family experiences and cultural images had laid this foundation before she could think or reason. No wonder thought and reason could not free her from the trap.

INTROJECTS

Perhaps the most easily understood and most commonly experienced structures are introjects. "Clean your plate," is a common phrase you may hear running through your mind when you sit down to dinner. That phrase is an introject. Your mother may not be there, but you still experience an internalized representation of her.

Introjects are internalized experiences of people in your life. It might be a specific person like a father, or a kind of person like a policeman or an accountant. This structure is the home and origin of all biases, prejudices, and judgments.

Introjects are common and a bit more concrete because individuals can usually identify the people and voices that have shaped them and continue to speak to them. In the absence of the actual person, this internal representation can be just as powerful at producing guilt or motivation.

Regardless of whether it's a paradigm, archetype or introject, each of our minds have been actively building structures since birth. Without asking permission, our brains filter, analyze and organize data and experience to construct internal realities.

Why does this matter? *Because new data will fail to integrate into a person's experience if it conflicts with an existing structure.* It will be rejected, categorized as false, or unavailable. In some cases, the senses will even disregard it as if it does not even exist.

The structures in people's souls are their picture of reality, and all new experiences must encounter these structures to be assigned a place in their minds.

Jane had a picture of herself, of men, and of God. None of the words and ideas that she had heard or read had the ability to change those structures, and since the structures remained unchanged, her experience remained unchanged.

The important men in her life had given terribly confusing, but consistent, messages about her body, her sexuality, and their acceptance of her. Her father had been the one who had fused this terrible internal representation of sexuality to her value and her acceptance.

Because these structures or introjects formed early in life and had been built by the "all-important" father, the messages about sex and value were anchored to her very sense of identity. Her internal picture of herself remained unchanged. Her thoughts, emotions, and behaviors remained unchanged. That is, until they changed.

THE FIRST STEP TOWARD CHANGE

When Jane had an encounter with her heavenly Father, her journey began to take a turn. God began to do more than inform her about her need to change. He began to deconstruct a lifetime of internal representations.

Through a personal encounter with God, the aspect of her structures that filtered out input began to slowly allow in new images. For Jane, this was the beginning of real change. A structure's power extends beyond its ability to tell someone how to experience reality. It also filters out any input that might contradict how they see reality.

The first step to inviting change is to get past the gate-keeping function of internal structures. Like the acrobat instructing his young students, instigators of change must do more than provide input. Often, they must overcome ingrained culture.

The bull's-eye for communication that changes lives is painted around the structures that have been built over a lifetime. These are the governing forces that decide what to do with information and sensory input when it comes into the mind. While the target of change is to begin eroding or even tearing down these structures, it is important to understand these thought processes.

Providing people more information, new information, or confrontational information has no power at all to reach structures—because structures capture, subjugate, and re-organize all incoming information before change can take place. It is for this reason that many forms of communication don't produce effective change and, as we will see in later chapters, can actually increase the strength of these structures.

Before diving into how to change structures, it's important to understand two truths. The first is this: *Structures came into existence through experience—not through information. In the same way, structures can be changed through experience—far more effectively than through providing information.*

> "THOUGHT PROCESSES CANNOT BE CHANGED BY NEW THOUGHT CONTENT. IT TAKES A PROCESS TO CHANGE A PROCESS."

Wilderness-based treatment programs are designed around the idea that experiences are more effective change agents than sitting in a classroom. Programs like this place people in circumstances where they have real life encounters with survival skills and self-protection. This forces them into having a real-life experience that challenges their structures.

The second truth is that *thought processes cannot be changed by new thought content. It takes a process to change a process.* Structures are not torn down simply by receiving helpful data. They are torn down by questions, interruptions, non sequiturs, and a variety of other process-based teaching approaches we'll look at in future chapters.

12 KEYS TO CHANGING A STRUCTURE

The Holy Grail of change is to gently erode a structure. This must be done gently because structures are well-defended. Attack too aggressively, and recipients will dismiss or resist the change you are trying to invoke. As a structure begins to weaken, it's important to put in place new thoughts or ideas the mind can use to rebuild a new structure. These new internal representations are always the goal when talking about meaningful and long-term change.

1. **First and foremost, a level of rapport is important.** If you are new to a person or group of people, it's difficult to tear down a long-held structure. In an upcoming chapter, I will guide you in building relationships with your audiences and readers. This is especially important if the structure you challenge affects their Christian beliefs.

If affecting change is your goal, you must be willing to relate to people—especially if you hope to address deep structures about love and value. Engage with people, walk with them, and get to know them. Let them know you. You do yourself no favors as a communicator to hide your true self from the people you want to help.

2. **Second, it is crucial to identify the structure you want to change as well as the new structure you want to help build.** In the same way missionaries must understand the culture they are entering and the shift they want to bring, you must know the territory on both sides of the change.

3. **When you want to start changing a structure, start by questioning everything with respect.** It is important to express value for the person or audience while questioning their long-held beliefs. Look for and question the underlying assumptions of the structure you want to change. Don't tell; ask. Let the listeners gently begin to doubt, so they can begin to let go. Their underlying assumptions are the building blocks of their structure, so just keep planting question marks.

4. **If possible, find logical fallacies in their underlying assumptions.** If not logical fallacies, then at least find incongruences, or inconsistencies, in their beliefs. Amplify the foundations of the assumption just enough to allow the incongruences to become evident. If you can, avoid pointing them out directly. The less you seem like you are trying to bludgeon their beliefs, the less they will put up their defenses.

5. **Use confusion to their benefit.** Rather than providing specific points, just chip away at foundations. Ask thought-provoking questions, and don't be afraid to let the questions marinate. Structures were built over time and repetition. The best a single teaching or conversation can do is leave your audience confused and needing to process.

6. **Give mental breaks.** If you are in a teaching setting, understand that it is mental work for your audience to reconsider long-held beliefs. Stop and tell a story. Tell a joke, particularly a joke that moves the audience toward change. Even if they can focus on the topic at hand for your entire time together, it is not to their benefit to do so. Let their minds breathe.

7. **Don't try to rebuild a whole structure for them.** Give your audience places to go, to read, or to listen. Give them directions of thought more than concrete ideas. Give them permission or freedom to engage in their own rebuilding process. Think of it like turning a ship; if you can change direction, the new course will eventually become clear.

8. **Empathize with your audience as you go.** Do not be haughty or too directive. They are working hard, and sometimes they are working in directions that may even feel "wrong." Remember their structures were the internal processes that defined their previous version of "right."

> "PEOPLE HAVE HAD THEIR STRUCTURES A LONG TIME AND YOU ARE IN SACRED TERRITORY TO BE TRUSTED ENOUGH TO CHALLENGE THEM."

Tearing down a structure can be as specific as helping someone who had an abusive father find a new picture of "Father," or as broad as moving someone from legalism to grace. In both cases, people have had their structures a long time and you are in sacred territory to be trusted enough to challenge them.

9. **Be kind.**

10. **Be persistent.**

11. **Listen.**

12. **And keep chipping away.**

Words are crucial, but the more powerful arenas of communication—ideas and structure—must be illuminated and then regenerated.

Is smoke coming out of your ears yet? Good! Your structures are being torn down. "Wax on. Wax off." Rebuilding the way *you* think changes the way you approach helping *others* think. Now, let's revisit words, the power they hold, and how to most effectively unleash their power to the logical, left brain.

STUDY GUIDE

KEY CONCEPTS

- We communicate with words, conceptualize in ideas, but we grow and change at the level of structure.

- A structure is an internal representation of our external world.

- Our structures filter out input that is inconsistent with already existing structures.

- The target of change in communication is to deconstruct and reconstruct structures.

- To deconstruct structures, questions, thought interruptions and unexpected language are far more effective than just providing new information.

SKILL BUILDERS

1. This week watch or read something from someone you know you disagree with. Listen for their structures and pay attention to your own. Note how your emotional responses indicate that the material violates your structures.

2. Listen for the voices of family members or teachers that may run through your mind. What kind of things do those voices say? Do they help you or undermine you? What do you experience if you challenge those voices?

3. If you have friends from other cultures (even if it is the same country), watch for how they see the world differently than you do. Ask them about values like family and education. Ask them about how they see life and death. Listen for their structures and as you do, pay attention to your own.

CHAPTER 4
HOW YOUR WORDS CAN UNLEASH POWER

*As handy as words or labels can be they short circuit observation.
Explanations are like words only more so.*
—Efan, Lukens, and Luken

You keep using that word. I do not think it means what you think it means.
—Inigo Montoya, *The Princess Bride*

The entire state of Hawaii began to prepare for a fiery end to life as they knew it. On January 13, 2018, a Hawaii State Emergency worker sent out the warning that all residents were to prepare for an inbound intercontinental ballistic missile. Later this worker said he was certain the events of the drill were real, and he did what he was trained to do. Unfortunately, this worker had missed one word in the communication—*Exercise.* The other employees had heard it. The one with his finger on the warning button had missed it. *One word.*

In the last chapter, we discussed the importance of words as building blocks of communication. They hold immense power. The patterns of our language connect to the patterns of our mind, and as such, a single word or a single omitted word can completely change the meaning of a sentence. If it changes the meaning of a sentence, it can change the direction or function of a specific thought process.

Like a tree that grows in an entirely different direction after being struck by lightning, so can our train of thought switch tracks with the skillful use of the right word or language pattern.

I stopped today to peruse a table piled high with Girl Scout Cookies. The young girls behind the table asked if I was interested in buying their wares.

"I think so," I said. "I am just trying to decide what I need."

> "WORDS CAN BE TRIGGERS, SETTING OFF A CHAIN REACTION OF THOUGHT."

The youngest salesperson at the table perked up. At nine years old, she eyed me shrewdly and said, "I am glad you used the word *need* instead of *want*. At least you know you need these. So... how many of these do you need?"

I was taken aback at her skillful wordsmith-ery and complimented her on it.

She smiled slyly. She knew.

I bought a single box. The one I needed, of course. I think I won.

We must develop our skills with the tools at our disposal, and our tools are words. We must also learn that certain words in certain settings have immense power to open the heart and mind—including the logical, left brain.

Perhaps you've heard of the differences between the left and right hemispheres of the human brain. In short, the left hemisphere controls logic and analytical thinking. It's the side that goes to work when you balance your monthly budget, organize your Netflix queue or figure out the specifics of a home improvement project. The right brain is the side that loves music, poetry, and parables and often comes up with the home improvement project in the first place. Generally, one side is more dominant in each individual, but both sides are at work in everyone. We'll examine strategies for reaching both sides—and we'll start with the left brain and its most powerful tool—words.

Certain words have the power to evoke a reaction or to numb an audience. Words can be triggers, setting off a chain reaction of thought. Words can be keys to opening doors or perhaps securing doors that protect thoughts. Words can be medicine soothing the angst of a restless crowd, and words can be water satisfying the thirst of a parched soul or extinguishing the fire of a once burning heart. Words proven empty can numb the listener into hopeless resistance to listen any longer.

Used properly, like the acrobat used them, words can trigger thought processes and structure changes. Used improperly, as we saw in Jane's story in Chapter Three, they can even be harmful.

In this chapter, we will unpack our toolbox and discover the immense power of not just words, but word selection and, ultimately, our language patterns.

WORDS AS TRIGGERS

Combat veterans understand the idea of a "trigger." Their weapons have triggers that unleash the power of the projectile known as a bullet…and in most cases, their minds have triggers that they must learn to manage when they return to everyday life.

A trigger is a small stimulus that unleashes greater power. A well-chosen and rightly placed word is exactly that.

The use of a trigger on a weapon is intentional and fulfills a conscious purpose. In contrast, the trigger in the mind is often unconscious and involuntarily constructed. But if we will be *purposeful* and *intentional* with our words, they can be just as targeted and powerful as a bullet.

We must choose words on purpose, words we know will have an impact, and we must use them for a calculated effect. The visiting musician who uses the name of the city he is playing in knows that the carefully selected words, "Hello, Dallas!" evoke civic pride and a sense of connection that will produce a "spontaneous" audience reaction.

We name a sports team or a familiar slogan knowing that it connects us to a community and creates a sense of solidarity with our listeners. All these intentionally selected triggers communicate that we are all in this together.

Consider the various reactions unleashed by the following trigger words:

- Republican

- Democrat

- Sin

- Submission

- Repent

- Feminism

- Masculinity

- Gun control

As you read through that list, did you notice how each word can create a visceral response in a positive or a negative direction, depending on the audience?

What if we were to learn this as a skill? What if in our relationships—on stage and off—we learn to listen for the vocabulary of the people we engage? What if we don't only listen for the vocabulary, but we create a glossary in our minds? What if we learn the vernacular of the people and use it in our conversations?

A heart connection is closely connected with vocabulary. If the mention of the local sports team builds a connection, how much more can you connect with those around you by learning what matters to them? A good teacher might use an agrarian reference with a more rural crowd and a more cosmopolitan reference with an urban group. Similarly, consider the impact of an offhand reference to John Wesley when speaking to a group of Methodists.

On occasion when I speak through translators, I will listen for the non-English version of a word I may use often. Then I wait for a chance to use it instead of the English word. It often draws a warm response from a crowd, no matter how poorly I may pronounce it. Words designed to trigger comradery or connection can be a simple and effective tool if used naturally and sparingly.

Because words have specific meaning, a single word can trigger the mind to go in one direction versus another. The young Girl Scout keyed in on the not-so-subtle distinction between the word "want" versus the word "need."

It's similar to the words "have" versus "get." Parents who tell their children "tomorrow we *have* to go to Cleveland" may create a sense of frustration or even resistance. "Have to" implies obligation and requirement and those ideas often produce negative feelings and even resistance.

Whereas, parents who tell their children, "tomorrow we *get* to go to Cleveland" could produce a sense of wonder, excitement, or positive expectancy. While some of the difference could be conveyed in tone, the two words have entirely different meanings and can produce two opposite results.

Keep in mind that word selection not only produces results in your listeners, but it also reveals the posture of your own heart as a speaker, teacher, or writer. Part of what it means to "guard your heart" is to examine the language that you speak and learn what it tells you.

It is important to be aware of negative triggers too.

On my first visit to the Holy Land, I received a warning to avoid referring to myself as a Christian. The warning was not about hiding my faith. It was about respecting the fact that a group of 12th century Crusaders wearing the label "Christian" had ransacked Israel. Centuries later, the word "Christian" triggers something different to those living in the Holy Land than it does to me.

In another setting a friend of mine used an example from his early religious training. The school he attended didn't allow people to walk on the grass. He told this to a group and as soon as he said it, the whole room stiffened. We all felt it. His words had hit an invisible nerve.

"You guys aren't allowed to walk on the grass either, are you?" he asked, recapturing the moment, and moving on. His words had triggered a sore spot in every person in his audience.

Of course, words as triggers are generally cultural and situational. Try using the word "submission" in certain settings and see if you can feel the trigger squeeze. Interestingly, the same word in another setting may actually open people's minds.

Years ago in a training session, a friend of mine heard God tell her she was brave. When asked what God had said to her, she inserted a small but powerful edit to what God had said.

> **"OUR WORDS CREATE A PATHWAY THAT THE MIND USUALLY FOLLOWS."**

"What did God say to you?" I had asked.

"He told me to be brave." Something didn't sit right in her response.

"Did He tell you *to be* brave?" I pressed.

"No," she said a bit sheepishly and perhaps unconvinced. "He told me *I am* brave."

The power of one word over another is crucial. "Be brave" can create shame and fear, and the need for self-effort, but "you *are* brave" creates wonder and empowerment and the opportunity to discover something hidden in your heart.

Becoming a communication ninja begins with realizing that all communication is a two-way exchange. Learn the culture and vocabulary of your audience. Listen to commonly used words or ideas from those around you. Speaking people's language back to them is a powerful way to gain immediate and deep rapport.

WORDS AS KEYS

The year was 1995, and the Orlando Magic had fought their way to the National Basketball Association's Championship series against the Houston Rockets. Game one, the upstart Orlando team was up by three in the final minutes of the fourth quarter.

A six-foot, six-inch guard by the name of Nick Anderson went to the free throw line. In the waning moments of the game, this 70-percent free throw shooter missed four free throws in a row, ultimately costing Orlando the game and beginning their series with a loss instead of the seemingly guaranteed win. They lost the series and the next several years saw Nick Anderson's free throw percentage drop to 36-percent by 1998. This drop also affected his willingness to drive to the basket.

That single moment changed not only the outcome of a crucial game, but also Nick Anderson's career for years to come.

What happened? I believe the post-game interview held meaningful clues to the shift that affected years of his life.

"What happened out there, Nick?" came the dreaded question.

I don't remember his exact words, but they were something like this, "I took my first shot and I said, 'I am not shooting like myself.' Nothing would fall after that."

With all respect for him and the situation he found himself in, Nick Anderson told himself what to do. The words, "I am not…," became a statement his unconscious mind obeyed, and his free throws followed suit.

I have often wondered how it may have turned out differently if he had, after his first missed shot, told himself, "Wow, that's not me. I am a great free-throw shooter. I am going to be me for the next several shots."

Words have meaning, and they have the power to bring about whatever meaning we assign them. Our words create a pathway that the mind usually follows. What if Nick Anderson had reminded himself to *be himself* instead of telling himself that he *was not himself*?

On that day, his words became a key that locked a door holding his truest self hostage. Words as keys can open and close the doors of our mind.

Compare these two statements about trying new things:

a. *"The principles described here are time-tested, and everybody should be following them if they want the kind of success I have…"*

b. *"If things haven't been working the way you think they ought to, consider that another way might open up new possibilities..."*

Do these statements feel different as you read them? What internal reactions do you notice as you read each one?

The differences between the two statements are in the language patterns. The first is prescriptive and centers on the speaker. In some people, it could shut down the listening ear and even shut the mind. The second is an invitation and focuses on the hearer. It is an invitation to possibility.

In the first phrase, the word "should" is often a key that locks people out. While this may not be true for every listener, resistance is a common response to that word. Using the word "should" or other similar prescriptive words can lock the mind of a listener to any words that follow.

In the second phrase, the word "consider" is used. This is presenting the listener or reader with options, and most importantly, this phrase gives them power. "Consider" says that the hearer has choices and freedom to exercise those choices. The word "should" implies that perhaps you have a choice, but you would be wrong (bad, dumb, ignorant, etc.) not to choose the way the teacher suggests.

The exaggeration here draws attention to the different implications of two words. These implications affect people's immediate visceral reaction and as a result either lock their minds or open them.

Consider the simple difference between using a positive statement versus a negative one.

a. *"I always forget my keys."*

b. *"I will start remembering my keys."*

The first statement may be a true statement (though you *should* "never" say "always"), but if words have power, the first statement can maintain a self-fulfilling train of thought. The second statement is no less true, but the internal direction of that statement is toward change instead of describing a static problem.

Or consider...

a. *"You are always going to struggle with grief."*

b. *"Grief always reminds you of how much your loved one meant to you and, over time, you will experience it in new ways."*

The first statement may be an accurate way to describe the pervasive, long-term course of the grieving process, but it also sounds like a sentence to eternal suffering. The second is an offer to be human. The first can make someone feel trapped. The second, while still saying the same thing, offers a hopeful future.

Keys are precision instruments, and as we listen to our words we can always fine tune them. As Mark Twain said, "The difference between the almost right word and the right word is really a large matter—'tis the difference between the lightning bug and the lightning."

I had the privilege to illustrate this in a recent training experience. The trainees paired up to help each other hear God speak to them. One student asked God to "infiltrate" every part of her. She asked but seemed to struggle.

The thought popped in her mind that "infiltrate" was something you do with enemy territory, so she shifted the word, asking God to "permeate" every part of her instead. As she shifted her word, her experience also shifted. Immediately, she felt peace settle inside her spirit, and she ceased to struggle.

A key that is similar, but not the right key, cannot open a door. In the same way, our word selection can mean the difference between the lightning and the lightning bug when encouraging people to change.

LANGUAGE PATTERNS

In the last chapter, I mentioned that words are symbols. In and of themselves, they have no power, but the realities they represent can have significant meaning to listeners and readers. The meanings represented by words connect people to themselves and to one another. To really drive home this idea that word choice matters, I want to end this chapter by showing you some keys in our language used to describe freedom.

The target of this book is to help people lead others to change, to experience freedom. I mention in my first book, *Think Differently Live Differently: Keys to a Life of Freedom,* that freedom is a heavily counterfeited commodity.

Listen to the language patterns often used to move people toward freedom. You will hear the subtle but powerful difference between true freedom and behavior management. These arise from our heart as language patterns, and they connect to others through language.

Jesus came to set captives free. Strangely and far too commonly, we mix the message up and think He came so we would manage our behavior. When we expect people to change for God, it is humanism. When we convey how to access what God has done for people, it changes more than meaning. It changes their ability to change.

Consider the following language patterns when addressing transformation. A few shifts in language can change the weight and meaning of a message. If a message changes, then the impact on listeners changes.

Does the language of the speaker…

Describe things God wants *us* to do?

or

Describe things God has done *for us?*

Describe something God *wishes* we had?

or

Describe something God wants to reveal or restore to us that already exists?

Describe something that God calls us to *do?*

or

Describe something that is an expression of *who we are*?

Describe something *natural* (comes from our efforts)?

or

Describe something *supernatural* (comes from God)?

Urge you to use your will to initiate something?

or

Urge you to use your will to surrender to Someone?

Try to persuade you to act differently?

or

Offer to help you SEE differently?

In each pairing, the first phrase describes a subtle counterfeit while the second phrase describes a genuine pathway to freedom. Sometimes the difference between the two opposites is a single word. It becomes easier and easier to see the truth every time you look at it.

Communication is a bridge between human souls. It is a bridge that allows us to cross over the gap between us, reach the deep places of our fellow man, and invite them to bring themselves to the forefront. The strength and capacity of this bridge is derived from the quality and clarity of the bricks and the mortar: Words.

> **"COMMUNICATION IS A BRIDGE BETWEEN HUMAN SOULS."**

Words reveal internal structures. By becoming conscious of the words we use, as well as the words that those in our audiences use, we can better understand what has been built on the inside.

When we each become intentional about our words, then we are more prepared to allow God to speak through us and help others experience change. We can, in turn, build a bridge filled with rich connection and growth to others.

THREE LEVELS TO ENGAGING SCRIPTURE

One of the clearest examples of the power of words is Scripture—God's Word, the written words of the Creator of the Universe. History recounts multiple instances when this sacred text was used to either bring eternal life or physical death to thousands, all depending on its interpretation.

Even today, we live in a time when people often make one of two mistakes when understanding, using, and engaging with Scripture. On one side, they want to discard or discount Scripture in the name of compassion or "modern thought." This idea suggests that Scripture is an ancient document that brings no light to a modern age of science and technology. This is compounded by the fact that Scripture does not always address specific issues. Sadly, this ditch dismisses the Divine inspiration of Scripture and suggests that the God who designed science didn't realize the complexity and sophistication of the human race. It dismisses an all-knowing God.

The ditch on the other side causes people to adhere rigidly to Scripture in response to rapid and confusing cultural shifts. They believe that their interpretation of it is black and white with no room for deeper understanding or a shift in perspective. The people on this side want to adhere to the exact language, or a translation of an exact language. They hold onto what they believe like a stake driven into the ground, and they refuse to consider Scripture in any other light.

As is often the case in polarities, those on either side provoke one another to strengthen their position. They see the error of the other side, and dig in even deeper like a life and death game of conceptual tug-of-war.

Somewhere in the middle, meaningful thought and life-giving truth become the casualty. Instead, I suggest we allow ourselves to learn differently from Scripture. Specifically, I propose that we maintain a tight grip on the reality that Scripture is God-breathed and therefore always valuable for helping us to think, know, and instruct. At the same time, I would love for us as people of faith to think beyond only the language level of Scripture and allow the truth behind the language to form our thought processes. Even more specifically, I want to consider three levels at which we should allow Scripture to teach us.

LEVEL 1: WORDS FOR INSTRUCTION

Clearly the words of Scripture can and should provide us with instruction about values, morality, and how we can live healthy lives. In 2 Timothy 3:16, Paul says that Scripture is inspired, or breathed by God and, therefore, has value for instruction, correction, doctrine, and reproof. Simply put, it is legitimate to use the words of Scripture to know good and bad, right and wrong, and the ways God designed us to live.

Very few people would argue that the Ten Commandments no longer have any value. Whether describing legal guidelines ("Thou shalt not kill") or simply healthy mental and emotional living ("Thou shalt not covet"), the words of the Ten Commandments passage and many others can help us think clearly about the issues of life. The concern is when we only value Scripture at this level.

One of many showdowns between simple thinkers and Jesus was when a group of men brought a woman to Jesus who, as Scripture says, was "caught in the act" of adultery. They threw her at His feet and challenged Him at the language level of God's Word, Jesus' own Word.

"The law says she should be stoned to death," they challenged. "What do you say?"

Have you ever had your words used against you? When someone either misunderstood your intent or simply wanted to be spiteful and throw your words back at you regardless of what you originally intended? These men focused on the language, not the idea, and something became lost in the translation. These men had done exactly this when they challenged Jesus, the Living Word, with the intent and message of the Written Word.

This showdown gives us beautiful insight into both human nature and God's nature. Human nature regularly separates the meaning of words from thoughts, while God's nature is always consistent and congruent.

Jesus got inside those guys' heads and sent them off one at a time with very few words. "He who is without sin cast the first stone." His words got inside their thought processes and revealed their hearts. They left.

He looked at the woman and asked where her accusers had gone. When she stated the obvious—they had left—Jesus brought words and meaning back together.

"Neither do I accuse you," He said simply and sent her on her way with the power to live differently.

When we allow Scripture to only be understood at the language level, we separate the words from their meaning. Doing this increases the likelihood that we take the opposite stance of the Author of the Words. At some point, we must move beyond words and allow Scripture to inform our thought processes.

LEVEL 2: THOUGHT PROCESSES

The idea of thought process is sprinkled liberally throughout this book. Thought process is what our minds do with a thought once it enters our senses. Thought process must be differentiated from thought content. Thought content is simply the data or ideas we have in our minds.

One way to think about thought process is to consider optimism versus pessimism. These aren't only personality types; they are ways of thinking. An optimist and a pessimist can hear the exact same thing and process it in two different ways.

If Scripture informs our thought process and not only our thought content, then we begin to use our minds in new ways. Thinking differently is in fact the first target of Jesus' teaching, and it must be differentiated from merely thinking different. Thinking different means changing from one thought to another. Thinking differently means changing from one thought *process* to another.

Isaiah 55 tells us, "our thoughts are not His thoughts," but it goes on to specify, "our *ways* are not His *ways*." Our ways of thinking dictate how the actual thoughts will end up catalogued in our mind. The pessimist will file everything under fear; the optimist will file everything under "Whoa, that's going to be amazing!"

The *ways* that we think always dictate the pathway and landing place of *what* we think. If we allow Scripture to begin to inform our thought processes, we can take the law that tells us a woman caught in adultery should be stoned and somehow turn it into an opportunity to give life to her and release her from a man-made trap.

Another example of thought process is the warehouse versus nozzle model. Many people think the mind is a warehouse, as if the mind is only a place for storage. Words come in, words are stored, and words are recalled. That is itself a thought process. Whatever words come in, passive storage is one possible way to process them.

What if instead we allowed the mind to be a *nozzle*—like the attachment on the end of a garden hose? What if God provides

> **"HUMAN NATURE REGULARLY SEPARATES THE MEANING OF WORDS FROM THOUGHTS, WHILE GOD'S NATURE IS ALWAYS CONSISTENT AND CONGRUENT."**

a constant supply of thought, and we could attach our minds to the "new-every-morning" mind of Christ? Now instead of passive storage, we become an active participant in the distribution of God's love and life. We receive, we contain and we broadcast.

As teachers and speakers, our methods always imply thought process. If we teach so that our hearers will memorize and store up ideas for the test that will come later, we implicitly teach the warehouse process. If we both exemplify and facilitate a "hear as you go" process, we implicitly teach the nozzle instead. Both are thought processes.

If we use the words of Scripture but do not develop the thought processes we see in Scripture, we can turn words intended to give life into words that give death. When we begin to develop the thought processes of Scripture, it is more likely that a Scripture-sculpted life will be the result.

And what of the world we live in? What if we learn to think like the Author of Scripture but still live with a worldview compiled by our senses?

LEVEL 3: PARADIGMS AND WORLDVIEW

The Bible, from Genesis to Revelation, gives us a picture of the nature of the world that God designed. To fully allow Scripture to inform the path and strategies of our life, we must let it tell us the nature of reality. We must let it reform the internal structures that we have spent a lifetime forming.

> **"TO FULLY ALLOW SCRIPTURE TO INFORM THE PATH AND STRATEGIES OF OUR LIFE, WE MUST LET IT TELL US THE NATURE OF REALITY."**

While these paradigms are not often stated explicitly in Scripture it is important that we look behind the stories and scenes to see how the Bible exposes these sweeping constructs of reality. It is these paradigms that provide the life-giving soil from which we can harvest the thought processes and language of the Bible.

If we miss the paradigms of Scripture, we will always misapply the instructions of Scripture. From beginning to end, we see a worldview in the Bible that is very different from the worldview of a modern Western thinker. Let's look at some examples.

INTEGRATED NATURAL AND SPIRITUAL REALMS

In every account in the Bible, the spiritual world and the natural world are interwoven. We see this from Genesis, where physical trees bear spiritual fruit, to Revelation, where the New Heavens and New Earth invade the existing realms. Every miracle and every cultural development that involves God's intervention is, in essence, the two worlds reintegrating. Because we stand in the natural realm and have spent a lifetime learning how to learn with our natural senses, we view reality primarily from a natural worldview. As a result, we see Divine intervention almost as a magic trick, a moment in time where a surprising and unexplainable event (by natural explanations) appears before our eyes.

The integrated worldview makes these kinds of events more "natural." Our minds' explanations move from the "magic-trick" conceptualization to more of the picture we see standing by the sea: It is expected that sand gets wet. The sand closest to the shore is more sea-soaked and the constant washing of the waves renews the moisture of the sand.

When we begin to allow the Bible to inform our view of the nature of reality, we see the "miraculous" as a natural result of the waves of the Kingdom lapping at the shore of our planet. We also better understand how to be participants in trying to splash the dry places in which we dwell.

THE END FROM THE BEGINNING

What is God up to? If we view reality from the position of our daily lives in a natural world, it may seem that He is helping us sometimes and ignoring us at others. This view can be shaped by either optimism or pessimism.

The Bible gives us a better understanding of God's unfolding plan, if we allow it to inform our paradigm. Drawing paradigmatic thinking from Scripture only comes when we broaden our views and look at the big themes that are constant in the Bible.

One way to understand God's unfolding plan is to see that He is a One-Become-Two-Become-One sort of God. Out of the singularly existent heavens, He creates the heavens and the earth and, through man's dominion and connection to God, bids that the two realms become one. From His singular nature, He issues forth man, and then pursues man in such a way that the two of them might enter a "become one" type of relationship. Out of the one man, Adam, He takes the woman, Eve, and then urges the two of them to become one. This beginning and ending as "one" can show us a beautiful aspect of God's pursuing restorative Nature. He creates the end from the model of the beginning.

Another way to understand this idea is found in Isaiah 46:10. Isaiah tells us that God "declares the end from the beginning." One paradigm could tell us that God predicts the future, but the overarching story of Scripture shows us that God uses the model of the beginning to call into existence the final state of things. One become two, restored again to one.

What is God up to? In the big picture, He is calling back into existence what once was. It is easier to participate in God's plan if we recognize this paradigm.

HEAVEN TO EARTH

Children generally think of their family from the perspective of the immediate moment and usually from the framework of their own needs. Children who have grown up to become parents realize that a larger story prevails over generations of family. Our relationship to Scripture is similar. The more mature we become in our faith, the more we understand we are part of God's much larger plans.

God existed before us, and His plan includes us, but we are not the beginning or the end. Because we have only lived on earth, we think from earth to heaven as if that is the flow of all things. We store up our treasures in heaven so that someday we can go get them. We help people who are residents of earth to ensure a home in heaven. These can be the thoughts of earth bound humans with internal structures drawn from a religious past.

God, however, has always seen it the other way around. From the heavens, He considered and then created the earth. From the heavens, He sent heavenly beings to the earth. From the heavens, He—Himself—incarnated into the earth. When the veil was torn in two in the temple at the moment of Jesus' death, we might see that as people gaining access to the heavens, but the events that followed showed that God saw it the other way around. After the veil was torn, the dead bodies of the saints came alive again and walked around Jerusalem testifying about the Kingdom of Heaven. It would appear that more than people gaining access to the heavens, the heavens obtained full access to the human realm.

This shift from thinking heavenward from the earth to seeing earthward from the heavens is another constant theme in Scripture. It reminds us that the heavens are the source of the earth, not the other way around. In the same way, the world inside us is not yet the world around us, but the more congruent they become, the more we can be free and help others on the same path.

We have seen in this chapter that words are powerful. They can be triggers and they can be keys. Used wisely they can lay the tracks that guide the train of thought to the intended station. We also see that words, separate of thought processes and paradigms, could become lifeless or life-taking. Words are the building blocks of thinking and the building blocks of learning.

We have been working hard at thinking about thinking and learning about learning and we're not done yet! Words are crucial, but the more powerful arenas of communication—ideas and structures—must be brought to mind and then brought to regeneration. Now that we've seen how words unleash power, let's turn our attention to the whole brain—how it hears and how it filters what it hears. Learning these two things allows us to be one very effective agent of change.

STUDY GUIDE

KEY CONCEPTS

- Words are symbols that are only as powerful as their attached meaning.

- Words are keys that open or lock people's hearts or minds.

- Words are triggers that unleash the power in a listener.

- Words create pathways the mind will follow.

SKILL BUILDERS

1. Try to describe your spiritual beliefs without using the typical language of your religious culture.

2. This week work on precision. Try to find words that describe precisely what you see or feel. For example, instead of saying, "I'm happy," use words like "content," "overjoyed," or "warm." Instead of saying, "I'm sad," try words like "grieving," "empty," or "morose."

3. This week pay attention to your self-descriptive words. Do you use negatives ("I never do that right") or positives ("I can do better")? Whenever you find yourself using a negative, try changing it to a positive. Ask yourself what changes when you do so.

4. This week listen to other people describe themselves. Do they use Identity phrases such as "I am very critical," or behavior phrases like "I tend to criticize"?

CHAPTER 5

A USER'S GUIDE
TO THE BRAIN

*What is real? How do you define "real?" If you're talking about what you can
feel, what you can smell, what you can taste and see, then "real" is simply
electrical signals interpreted by your brain.*
—Morpheus, *The Matrix*

We do not see the world as it is. We see the world as we are.
—*The Talmud*

Before you delve into this chapter, STOP and put the book down. Trust me,
you will love this assignment. Get online and search "Daniel Simons selective attention test video." Follow the prompts until you have completed the
assignment, then come back and continue. Don't worry, I'll wait....

Back already? Great. Here was my experience:

The first time I watched that video, I was in a classroom setting. The assignment was to pay close and careful attention to the movement of a basketball passed among a group of people dressed in white. The assignment was
simple, and I was determined to get it right because I knew there was some
sort of trick to the assignment.

I faithfully and painstakingly counted each pass, not wanting to miss the
obvious. I focused, and I counted. Fourteen passes, I was sure of it. Not wanting to get fooled, I absolutely got fooled.

I'll never forget as we all gave our answers as to what we saw, the instructor asked the question: "You guys did a great job counting the passes, but did you see the gorilla?"

I narrowed my eyes. Not only did I begin to doubt the speaker (and quite honestly question his character!), but I also began to make assumptions about what I had missed. I figured they must have subtly sneaked in a gorilla in some peripheral way, providing a tiny glimpse, knowing that we were so focused, we wouldn't see it.

Then they showed the video again.

The gorilla had not been hinted at in some subtle sleight-of-mind sort of way. It had strutted right into the middle of the screen, stood among the players, and pounded its chest, doing all it could to draw attention to itself. Dead center, as big as life, screaming for attention.

I don't know about you, but the first time I watched the video, the gorilla had passed by right in front of me, in full view, and I had stared right at him. Focusing on the image, I did not see the most glaring and obvious part of the picture...until I did.

I had missed the obvious. And it seemed that 99% of the people in the room had missed the gorilla too. I was so glad I wasn't alone!

My brain had done its job well.

THREE BRAIN FILTERS

Everyone's brain has a mission from the moment it begins to operate. It has the overwhelming task of organizing input. It does not ask for permission; that would defeat its purpose. It works painstakingly, unconsciously, outside of an individual's awareness. Organize, organize, organize.

Unlike the sonar-guided dolphins, humans do not send out sounds. Instead, we send out *senses*. We send out our information gatherers—our five senses—to do their jobs. Every bit of data in our environment approaches our senses, insisting to be considered.

Immediately following birth, those senses begin to read the world. Our brains face the immense task of taking all our sensory input and creating an organization inside our mind. It does this so that we can know how to interact with our world.

The challenge is that our senses are taking in *millions* of bits of information. Scientists estimate our brains take in two- to eleven-million bits of data *every second!*

The brain must take all that data and do something with it to keep us from being overwhelmed every single moment of every day. The brain has multiple processes to sort through all these bits and only give us what we can handle. Amazingly, with all this data, the average brain can only handle *126* bits of data per second. Only 126 bits per second! That's like enjoying the beach one teaspoon of sand at a time. This is what the brain does. It spoon-feeds us from a banquet table.

Similar to dolphins, our brains sift through the data received and develop structures that allow us to navigate the world. Early on, those structures function to *sift out* input in order to prevent the brain from experiencing overload.

One of the first tasks of the brain is to decide what we don't see. Again, without permission, our brains start to develop a kind of "intentional" blindness.

Millions and millions of bits of data come in, only 126 receive awareness. That means that as individuals, we miss infinitely more than we perceive. Without even considering the idea that we live in a world with invisible spiritual realities, our brains leave out more than they let in.

> "SINCE WE SEE EVERYTHING WE SEE, IT'S EASY TO ASSUME WE SEE EVERYTHING THERE IS TO SEE."

Think about the room you're in right now. What sights, smells, sounds, tastes, touches have you simply—and completely—ignored as you've been reading this book? A cobweb in the corner, the sound of the air conditioning, the smell of soap, the taste of chocolate, the warmth of your cat lying on your lap—these all may have gone unnoticed on a conscious level.

Since we see everything we see, it's easy to assume we see everything there *is* to see. It's easy to assume that we sense everything there is to sense. As our brains filter out millions of bits of data, we convince ourselves that we see the world around us in its entirety. The brain's ability to filter millions of bits of data always trumps the ego's certainty that it knows everything. The problem is our egos don't tell us that our brain always wins.

Our brains filter out or organize this data so we can think clearly. Sadly, this clarity comes at the cost of objective accuracy. As we saw in Chapter Three, the mind builds structures of the world around us, like the dolphins who create internal sonar imagery. Unlike the dolphins, our structures are built not on objective sound waves but on pre-filtered perceptions and interpretations of sensory data.

As we come to understand these filters, we stand a better chance of being intentional in building and changing these structures in our own minds as well as in the minds of others.

DELETION

[1]Deletion is the filter that hid a demonstrative gorilla from me right in plain sight. The first filter the brain uses is deletion. It is a process by which we selectively perceive certain dimensions of our experience and exclude others.

Like the black tape over elements of a photograph, the brain practices deletion prior to perception. Simply put, we don't just see something and look away, we just *do not see it*. Deletion is responsible for the way one person can view the same thing as someone else and see something entirely different.

My wife and I frequently shop together, walking the same aisles in the same light, our eyes hitting the same objects as we go. Either one of us can call attention to something that the other has looked at and not seen. I have often said I would love to walk through a store with her eyes. We see different things because we see differently. We see differently because our internal structures delete different things. I see gadgets. She sees beauty. Not that I don't see beauty, I just see gadget-y beauty, and she sees aesthetics. She sees color and form and lines. I see hinges and clever construction ideas.

Deletion is the process that preselects what will be allowed past our sensory gatekeepers. It safeguards our brain from being overwhelmed, but it also prevents our brains from being fully informed.

Like the other filters discussed here, deletion becomes increasingly fine-tuned as we age. Selective attention and confirmation bias develop over time as the brain deletes certain things that do not fit its presets.

The deletion filter suggests that great learners and great teachers must be aware that they have only a very limited view. As a result, all meaningful learning includes new information as well as expanding the ability to see.

---

1 Richard Bandler and John Grinder. *The Structure of Magic: A Book about Language and Therapy*. Palo Alto: Science and Behavior Books, 1975.

GENERALIZATION

Generalization allows us to view many things at one time by grouping them into one category.[2] As the brain develops, it simplifies sorting through data by putting large quantities of data into general categories. All prejudices, judgments, and preconceived notions are a result of generalization.

Generalization is the process by which elements, or pieces of a person's model, get detached from their original experience and come to represent an entire category.

I once worked in a music group led by a man who looked just like a friend of mine from college. My friend from college was laid back with a great sense of humor. The leader of our group had neither quality. He was intense and serious about getting our music right. It took me a few weeks to stop interacting with him as if he had the same characteristics of my old friend. I had generalized him into a category, and all my interactions with him were guided by my internal structure, until they were not.

I constantly hear generalization at work when I sit down with clients who mutter the phrases, "Oh, you know women…," or "Oh, you know men…." It helps me know they have generalized by gender, and I see part of my job is to help them develop more sophisticated and increasingly accurate categories.

As teachers, we must recognize that we have generalizations and we must keep an eye out for them in our minds and hearts. It significantly undermines our influence when we speak or write from a generalization that our audiences or readers do not hold. Regional prejudice, gender expectations, and disagreements about social mores all result in an audience believing that a speaker is tone deaf.

We must also know that our listeners and readers have generalizations they do not see as generalizations. They see them as truth. Helping people become more sophisticated while expanding their senses in the moment is an important part of teaching people out of their categorizations.

DISTORTION

Earlier we saw that Jane had a variety of experiences with men. Many of the men she had known had treated her with respect and kindness and even with appropriate boundaries. Sadly, Jane rarely saw decency for what it was. When a man had been kind to her, she experienced his kindness as a come-

---

2 Ibid.

on. When a man had set a boundary, she experienced it as a rejection of her as a woman. Her mind had developed a filter that had distorted all interactions with men.

Distortion bends and batters input until it fits more easily into internal structures that we have already developed and committed to.[3] When people misunderstand us in a way that fits their expectations, but that doesn't reflect our actual expressions, we encounter distortion. They're bending our meanings to fit their preset understanding.

Distortion, like deletion and generalization, makes the brain's job easier. Specifically, it prevents the brain from having to work very hard to develop new structures. All three of these filters prevent good learning, but this one stealthily convinces a listener that they have learned something new when they have not, or worse, that they already knew what the speaker said.

While intentional distortion happens and must also be addressed, a good communicator must recognize that unconscious distortion is the enemy of having a new thought process. Clarity and specificity in communication is important because the mind is prone to distort.

> "THE MIND CREATES THE STRUCTURES THAT WILL GUIDE, INFORM, AND TELL PEOPLE HOW TO NAVIGATE LIFE."

Distortion is not a specifically negative process. The mind's ability to distort is the same process as the mind's ability to shift and make changes. It is a subset of the mind's flexibility, so without it, we would not be able to imagine things we have never seen or experienced. Distortion creates the flexibility that allows for change from one model to another new model.

As communicators, our clarity matters as we face this unconscious nemesis. And sometimes, clarity is not enough. Sometimes the use of precise *and* unusual language gives us the best chance to pierce the armor of distortion and allow our listeners' brains to hear a new thing. I used the word "structure" before explaining it in Chapter 3. I did this to prevent distortions from operating.

The mind applies deletion, generalization, and distortion and a few other filters to everything the senses pick up. In conversation, in learning, and even

---

3 Ibid.

in leisurely viewing entertainment, these filters are always active. The mind feverishly builds structures to make sense of and organize reality. The mind creates the structures that will guide, inform, and tell people how to navigate life.

The unconscious mind takes in more than the conscious, so the filters are less stringent. The unconscious mind sorts through implications or the various meanings of the sensory field. By its very definition, people are not immediately aware of the process which will eventually dictate how they see, how they think, and how they ultimately decide what is true.

Let me say it another way. While you are not paying attention your unconscious mind is deciding for you what you will and will not see, or hear.

UNCONSCIOUS EXPERIENCE

Simplification is the goal when facilitating change. The mind works to take an overwhelming task and make it manageable, all without asking the owner's permission. Asking permission would merely be one more form of input, so the brain handles the organization on its own. This activity is labeled as *unconscious,* which is, by definition, outside of awareness. It is these unconscious processes that so often filter and shape incoming data. The unconscious takes in and filters out data.

One of the most important implications of "internal structures" is that communicators must make their messages stand out to get through all the filters. Anything that is out of the ordinary or surprising to the mind can help our communication land in the minds of our hearers and readers.

By the way, had you wondered whether it was a man or a woman inside the gorilla suit?

Non sequiturs, words, or ideas that seem to jump the track of the train of thought, to catch the unconscious mind's attention, are all good tools. Another technique is the sudden interruption of the thought process with a one-liner or side observation.

It's also important to point out that the longer speakers speak, the longer they run the risk of their listeners checking out. Therefore, it's a good idea for speakers to interrupt themselves and their flow so listeners' minds can stop and check in.

Where is your mind right now? As you read this, are you needing to check in?

The unconscious mind takes in many elements of communication that the conscious does not. It asks questions like: Was the speaker smiling? Did he seem kind? Who did he look at, and who did he seem to *avoid* looking at?

This peripheral data is taken in and experienced as impressions such as, "He seemed like a nice guy" or "Something didn't feel right about that." Those kinds of senses are harder to put into words but are still no less part of the learning process.

Con men and predators learn to be charming for a reason. Whether they know it consciously or not, the unconscious impressions they make in communication affect how much of the communication gets through. If the source is trusted, the unconscious mind opens the gates a bit wider. Creating an impression is as much a part of the communication process as is the formation of ideas and words.

The other ways that unconscious learning impacts us all is that we see the "way" speakers do their jobs and what they believe about teaching. In other words we often pick up the "covert" communication unconsciously. Recognizing and harnessing these issues of unconscious learning are crucial because unconscious learning faces fewer filters and builds deeper structures.

So many factors influence the development of these internal structures that an entire book could be devoted to this. Our target is change rather than developing a comprehensive list. The most important concept in this chapter is that all this takes place as a natural function of the brain.

The brain, in its effort to make sense of the world and organize the overwhelming amounts of sensory input coming at each of us, filters millions of bits of data down to 126. These 126 bits then form a picture or an internal representation of the world that can be understood and managed. Our brains are pretty brilliant aren't they?

THREE STRUCTURE-BUILDING TOOLS

Rather than view the brain as an obstacle to helping people change, let's consider it a roadmap of the territory in which communication must travel. The brain is simply doing its job. When we understand this, it can work with us and for us instead of against us.

Old dogs can be taught new tricks, but the internal structures will resist them. Only those who know how to reach and influence these structures will succeed in new training for aging canines.

As these internal representations of reality grow stronger, changing them becomes more difficult. Experiences that most build these structures have certain characteristics. By looking at some of the structure-building tools, we can learn to use them on purpose.

REPETITION

The consistency with which someone encounters an idea or an experience, convinces their inner self that the idea is actual reality. Repetition is many times the key to true learning. However, repetition doesn't just mean repeating words.

Let me say it another way. Every time we turn on the light switch, the room lights up. This experience builds unspoken expectation. We do not realize how much we have come to expect the light to come on when we hit the switch until the moment we hit the switch and it stays dark. The visceral reaction we have to the lack of light reveals how much we have come to believe that flipping a switch creates light. That's "just the way it is."

Childhood experiences that stay constant build in that same kind of unconscious expectation. This is true whether the experience is positive or negative. People learn to trust words when the people around them follow through on their words. People learn to live with negative expectancy when the people around them don't follow through. This "solid" feeling on the inside about what to expect is a way that people experience these structures. Consistency mixed with the rest of these tools build strong expectations.

EXPERIENCE

What we experience always has more impact than the words we hear. Emotions or even fragrances are experiential. They produce an immediate impact on the nervous system. Words have to be translated through the cognitive process whereas experiences bypass the defense system.

One adage states, "People may not remember what you say, but they will remember how you made them feel." This is because overt communication is filtered through cognitive processes. Covert communication makes impact.

If we say something repeatedly and do the opposite repeatedly, people believe our actions more than our words. We teach our listeners and readers hypocrisy and mistrust. That experience will quickly negate any accompanying language.

When someone has built an internal structure through experience over time, it is unlikely that words alone could ever make a dent in their souls. In instances like this, our communication is more likely to bring about change if it involves experience and not only words.

INTENSITY

Trauma is a specialty in the counseling world because of the unique ways it lodges in the human soul. Trauma is the damage done when someone has an intense experience of violation, pain, or fear. The level of trauma is directly proportionate to the level of intensity of the violation, pain, or fear.

In the same way, learning that creates internal realities is a response to the intensity of the experience that facilitates the learning. That's why intensive experiences like retreats or summer camps can leave a deep mark on people.

Years ago, I had an automobile accident. A car behind me slammed into the right side of my car as I made a right turn. As I turned, I heard screeching brakes and felt a powerful impact on my right side. For months, every time I heard the screech of tires, I winced on my right side. I had "learned" what screeching tires meant. In fact, my nervous system knew it whether I wanted it to or not.

> "LISTENERS ARE MORE IMPACTED WHEN THEY HAVE AN INTENSE EXPERIENCE—NOT WHEN THE SPEAKER DOES."

Conversely, low-impact or low-intensity experiences leave no marked shift in people. We often remember a great meal or a terrible meal. They both have intensity, but we rarely remember average meals.

It is important for speakers to know that intense emotion in their voice does not necessarily make for more impactful communication. Listeners are more impacted when they have an intense experience—not when the speaker does.

Understanding how the brain filters input and then learning tools we can use to bypass these filters allows us to deliver our message more clearly and effectively. These filters are incredible but it is imporatant to know that they operate in a context. The mind operates in a dance with our feelings and our will. Let's take a look at the soul—at our minds, wills, and emotions—so we can get a better picture of exactly how people receive.

STUDY GUIDE

KEY CONCEPTS

- The brain functions to organize your world and it doesn't ask your permission.

- The brain filters out and changes input to fit into preexisting belief systems.

- Experience, repetition, and intensity build internal structures, filters, and lenses.

SKILL BUILDERS

1. If you skipped the exercise at the beginning of this chapter, be sure to look up and watch Daniel Simons' selective attention test video.

2. This week as you listen to others, see if you can identify a way they see the world that is different from the way you see it.

3. For a day, assume that you have missed amazing things in your ordinary life as you drive to work, where you work, or in your neighborhood. What is the most amazing thing that you have regularly missed?

4. This week in conversation, see if you can tell from other people's responses if they heard what you wanted them to hear, or if they imposed their own experience on your conversation.

CHAPTER 6

THE MIND, WILL AND EMOTIONS – HOW PEOPLE RECEIVE

The best teacher is the one who suggests—rather than dogmatizes—and inspires his listener with the wish to teach himself.
—Edward G. Bulwer-Lytton

Reading furnishes the mind only with materials of knowledge; it is thinking that makes what we read ours.
—John Locke

One of the greatest limitations to effective, transformational communication is the assumption that teaching is simply the transfer of information.

Imagine a potter sitting in front of a large lump of clay, describing *to* the clay the principles that can turn it into a pot. With words alone, the clay would remain motionless and eventually the potter would get frustrated as nothing happened.

I've never fired a clay pot myself, but I appreciate that potters have been creating clay pottery for thousands of years. Museums hold archeological finds of pottery, sometimes perfectly preserved in their original formation even though the potters who cast them are long gone.

When the ancient potters cast their creations, they clearly understood what it took to make a long-lasting vessel. First, they had to find the right clay for the job. If the clay had too many impurities or simply lacked the proper makeup, the potter wouldn't be able to create a long-lasting vessel no matter what he did next. In the same way, none of us can meet our goals of bringing lasting change to our listeners if we don't know their makeup.

But after the potters discovered what they were working with, they weren't done. They still had to measure the clay's plasticity, sculpt it, fire it at the right temperature, and apply a proper glaze. All of those attributes affected the potter's ability to cast a perfect vessel.

> **"THE MIND IS THE COLLECTION OF LESSONS LEARNED, STRUCTURES DEVELOPED, AND PROCESSES ENGAGED."**

Of course, any of those actions required the potters to get their hands dirty. They had to press into, impact, and imprint the clay. They had to push against it, squeeze it, and move the clay into position at just the right moment. They had to fire it, maybe even paint it. They stepped back often, evaluating their work, before diving in again to work with the lump. Similarly, we must understand the make-up of our listeners if we want our communication to have long-lasting impact. We must understand the constitution of the soul if we want to instigate powerful change.

In *Language Structure and Change* by Jay Efran, Michael Lukens, and Robert Lukens, the authors devote an entire chapter to what they call the "The Myth of Instructive Interaction." They describe how every instruction is more than just transferred data—how the nervous system waits like a mound of clay to be molded and formed.

When it comes to transformational communication, we need a new model. In building that model, we must start by understanding the makeup of the clay we are molding: the human soul. For practical purposes, we will define the soul as the mind, the will, and the emotions. These parts play meaningful roles in the receptivity of a student or listener.

THE MIND

The mind is more than the brain. The brain is an organ, but the mind is what the brain *does*.[4] The mind is the collection of lessons learned, structures developed, and processes engaged. It is not only thought, but it is also belief and the methods for constructing and deconstructing beliefs. The mind is the overall mechanism that takes in, organizes, and builds our inside world.

Many of the chapters throughout this book are dedicated to understanding the mind. An entire book would still not be enough to help us adequately learn how to engage the mind effectively.

It bears repeating that the mind is far more than a storehouse for input. The mind is an adaptive processing machine. When it is understood and well-cared for, it can be a teacher's most important target. While the emotions and the will are gatekeepers (as we'll see), the mind is the machine at the center of this complex learning system. The mind uses any input provided to build whatever it decides to build.

THE WILL

American psychologist Milton Erickson told a story of watching a group of men trying to force a mule into a barn. As a young man limited by polio, he watched a group of strong men struggling to get the mule to move even an inch.

Finally, he asked the man organizing the failed effort if he could give it a try. The man looked at the group of strong farm hands struggling to move the mule a single inch and looked back at the frail young man.

"What have we got to lose?" he mused. "Give it a try."

Erickson moved to the side of the mule away from the barn and with a gentle tug gave a token attempt to move the mule *away* from the barn. Spontaneously and of its own free will, the mule bolted under its own power—right into the barn.

Erickson understood several things about the will that the farmhands did not. In fact, he understood things that are foundational to the kind of communication that changes people.

"Spontaneously and of its own free will" becomes a way to describe how a learner responds to someone who skillfully understands and handles the

---

4 Andrew Newberg, Eugene D'Aquill, and Vance Rause. *Why God Won't Go Away: Brain Science and the Biology of Belief*. New York: Ballantine Books, 2001.

human will. The strength of the learner is harnessed by the teacher and used for the learner's benefit.

While good humanity suggests that we deeply respect the free will of our fellow man, effective communication and a bit of Neuro-Linguistic Programming (NLP) may tell us that free will is not as common as one might think.

Mentalists who "predict" what card subjects may draw, or which number they might choose, usually say that they didn't *guess* what their subjects would do at all. Instead they subtly *told* them what to choose. Using subliminal cues and language patterns, mentalists make unconscious suggestions, allowing their subjects to believe they *choose* to respond a certain way. The outcome makes the mentalists look as if they read their minds or predicted the outcomes.

As surprised as people are to discover that they have been programmed to a certain response or response pattern, it is the sense of free will that allows people to move "spontaneously and under their own power" into a given state or choice.

In a moment of brilliance, P.T. Barnum in the movie *The Greatest Showman* convinces Phillip Carlyle to leave a life of assured position and affluence and join him in a life of unpredictable experiences and unstable finances. The song-and-dance number shows the two dialoguing about the "opportunity" to which Barnum invites the young playwright.

Scornfully, the young socialite says he is absolutely not interested. With a few clever lines, Barnum offers him some key items. First, he offers him life and laughter and freedom. They are things Barnum saw lacking in the young man's life and therefore provided the ideal attractant. But the key and ultimately the turning point for the young Mr. Carlyle is when Barnum ends his offer with a sly smile toward the camera and the line, "but I guess I'll leave that up to you." A close up on Carlyle's face shows the sudden shift when he is offered *freedom to choose*—and in a split-second he changes his mind. This movie moment rings true because it reflects a scenario we've seen happen in real life more than once.

In this scene, we witness two crucial elements of understanding and respecting the will in persuasive communication.

First, we see that people are moved and changed when it is their own desires or identities that are given voice. When speakers promote selfish gain or try to force their opinions, listeners often shut down. When speakers help listeners connect to what *they* want, or to who they really are, they feel helped. Their will responds positively.

Second, we see the importance of respecting a person's freedom to choose.

Freedom to choose creates a momentum of movement like Erickson's mule toward the barn. It does more than decrease resistance; it increases desire.

This principle is particularly important when the target of communication is for the audience to find greater levels of freedom. If any aspect of communication feels coercive to listeners, the actual offer is counterfeit freedom and contains no freedom at all.

Listen sometime to the specifics of language when people speak about freedom. Consider the following sentence where words *prescribe* freedom:

> *Jesus went all the way to provide freedom for you. You should do everything you can to live out the freedom He gives.*

Words that prescribe can often set up an unconscious resistance in listeners. The use of words like "should" or "ought to" or even worse, *attitudes* that prescribe, can often set up the same resistance as the triggers we discussed in Chapter Four. These words produce a sense of obligation that will often quench natural desires. How much better would it be to *describe*:

> *God has put in you everything you were created for. Therefore all of your desires are yours already. The only thing between you and the experience of your true self is what your mind tells you.*

The two keys to engaging the human will to move spontaneously—of its own free will, and under its own power—are connecting to the desires that already exist in listeners and readers and helping them know they are free to choose either way.

In the book of Proverbs, we read that if you "train up a child in the way he should go, when he gets old he will not depart from it." So often readers think this language tells us that the child has a required pathway. This places parents in a great state of fear and power posturing in order to fulfill this instruction. However, "the way a child should go" is as unique as a fingerprint. If we look to an external standard for how a child "should go" we may try to force her into a mold that can never fit.

What if "the way they should go" is more like a seedling that is born into the soul? Just as an oak tree "should" go the way of an oak, and a tomato plant "should" go the way of the tomato, a child should go the way of his or her created nature…not according to an external standard of performance.

Along with a child's—or anyone's—created nature is all the resident drives and desires that are woven into his or her fabric. Find those. Appeal to those. Connect the things you are verbalizing with the things that are organically growing inside your listeners. They will move toward their desires as you help them discover for the first time what they have already been wanting. Then offer them the chance to choose freely rather than to follow or obey. Let their wills feel powerful, and let the power of their wills move them toward the goal. Make them feel powerless, and they will resist or give in without genuine engagement.

THE EMOTIONS

Bill was a gifted thinker. He was using principles he had learned about the brain to make changes at work and help his co-workers and employees. He was frustrated though. For all the help he offered, he was encountering ungratefulness and even resistance from the very people he wanted to help.

He described to me the strategies and methods he was suggesting. I was amazed at how clear and accurate his insight was. He was truly offering help, but as I continued to listen, it became clear. While Bill understood some meta-perspectives, had a great thought process, and expressed many strategic ideas, he was missing one very important piece—the people.

While Bill saw the *issues* with clarity, he did not see *people* with clarity. In particular, he had not yet gained an understanding of what moved people. Having a clear path is not the same thing as having a desire to move down it. That desire relies on emotions.

> **"HAVING A CLEAR PATH IS NOT THE SAME THING AS HAVING A DESIRE TO MOVE DOWN IT."**

In my counseling practice, I have often said that people are far more driven by emotions than we realize, and I'm not referring to hysteria. Emotions are simply our primary drivers or movers. Even when people say that they are not driven by emotions, they usually mean they don't outwardly express their feelings. The decision to "not be driven by feelings" is usually driven by a feeling of fear or self-consciousness.

Feelings matter because they move people. Emotions drive the will. While the will makes choices, emotions set the context and the menu for the choices being made.

Not everybody is tuned in to their emotions, but this does not change the fact that emotions are their primary drivers. Ironically, awareness, or lack of awareness, of feelings does not change the level of influence that emotions have. Lack of awareness may make change more difficult or even make it difficult for people to understand themselves or how they act.

Lack of emotional awareness in a listener, reader, or audience might actually be an advantage to a communicator who is emotionally tuned in. The human soul speaks the language of emotions even when the mind doesn't. Learn to speak that language and you will increase the depth of your reach with people.

Imagine if Bill had said to his co-workers, "I can see that you have been working on this a long time. You must be really frustrated. I think I can help relieve your frustration. Maybe I can even help you have a little fun while increasing your effectiveness." How much more effective that would be? After all, good information that didn't reach the hearts of his colleagues could simply feel intrusive.

The excellent book, *How to Talk So Kids Will Listen and How to Listen so Kids Will Talk* by Adele Faber and Elaine Mazlish, emphasizes that the language of empathy reaches people. But often the language of empathy is not what we think.

Telling people about feelings is not necessarily the language of feelings. Advice, input, or explanations move away from feelings because they move the speaker into the mind. When you speak *from* the mind, you always speak *to* the mind.

Neil Anderson's classic book, *Victory Over the Darkness,* reminds us that mind speaks to mind and heart speaks to heart. It is important to learn the difference between language *about* emotions and the language *of* emotions. The language of empathy discovers and connects to the emotional side of people.

Language about emotions explains feelings. The language *of* emotions contains feelings. Language *about* emotions names and describes feelings; whereas, the language *of* emotions connects to the emotions of others. Watch how this could have helped Bill.

Making the mistake of talking *about* feelings, imagine that Bill speaks up. "There is a lot of anger in this room and maybe even some resentment. Let's all keep cool heads and think clearly about these issues." Here he has spoken about feelings.

Now watch how Bill could change the atmosphere of the room with the language of true empathy.

"Susan, you seem very frustrated, and I am sorry you have felt ignored here," he says, making direct and warm eye contact. "We are a team, and I would be sad to see us divided after we have all worked through so many other difficult situations. Resentments are hard, but we have worked through them before."

As mentioned above, empathic connection can be especially important when listeners are disconnected from their own emotions. The language of empathy can reach inside a soul and awaken feelings that may have laid dormant. Often when I tell the original Parable of the Acrobat, people identify with the acrobat and respond with tears. The language of empathy can connect and reach the place inside a man or woman where God wants to connect.

If emotions are drivers (and they are!), then understanding how to reach, impact, and give power to emotions is central for the communicator who wants to help people change. But let's not oversimplify this step.

We have all been in a setting where a speaker begins to tell an emotional story, and as they emote, we feel our own emotions respond. We feel their grief or their pain, and we respond emotionally. While this is a valid way to reach people, it is not the main thrust of this section. Utilizing our emotional state to help others feel may be helpful but should never be overdone or contrived. Most people know when a speaker is manufacturing emotions.

Instead, let's look at several other effective ways to benefit our listeners by connecting to their emotions. Specifically, let's look at the roles of validation, metaphor and parable, as well as vulnerability.

VALIDATION

One of the most important aspects of tapping into the power of emotion as a communicator is to understand and practice validation. Validation is the act of communicating that people are seen, heard, and valued. This is particularly important for people who struggle with emotional isues. They often feel isolated and self-impose emotional insulation because of shame. For these people, being seen and heard is important to their healing journey.

Over the last several years, I have begun to speak and write about the dynamics of abuse. Specifically, I have taught on the role and posture of each party in the cycle. The abuser, the victim, and the helper all fall into a fairly predictable pattern.

For the victim, the dynamic is that they are silenced, not believed, and in many cases, blamed for the abuser's lot in life. Because of this, they often fail to speak up and may even quietly disappear or continue to suffer in silence.

I have begun to write and speak on this topic, and as a result, have tapped into a silent tsunami of human pain. I am stunned at the number of people who have experienced abuse and reach out to tell me their story. They usually say that they finally feel understood. Once they know they are believed, their stories begin to cascade out.

They often say that being validated brings relief. Rather than share my emotions, I find that making a safe place for their emotions provides a context for real change. I do this by verbally giving validity to their experience and their personhood. When their picture of themselves and others has been so distorted, this experience makes a deep shift for them. Their internal representation of themselves and the trustworthiness of others has an opportunity to change. It, once again, shows that any time we validate others, we provide opportunity for change.

> **"YOU CAN EXPRESS VALUE FOR A PERSON EVEN WHEN YOU COMPLETELY DISAGREE WITH THEIR BELIEFS."**

I have seen that some people have a difficult time validating people with whom they disagree. It is crucial to know that you can express validation of the other person's experience without agreeing with their thoughts. You can express value for a person even when you completely disagree with their beliefs. Validation is the key to connection and it is not dependent on agreement.

METAPHOR AND PARABLE

I mentioned a few moments ago how often when people hear the original Parable of the Acrobat, they're brought to tears. In an upcoming chapter, I will share a time that story hit many listeners at once. The bottom line is that buried emotions can be released or engaged by using parable.

Many people are uncomfortable with their emotions and as a result have put defenses in place to keep themselves from feeling too much. The beauty of parable and metaphor is that it bypasses most of these mechanisms. Listeners don't have cognitive filters in place to separate the story from their own feelings, so while parables are processed by the mind, they are accessed by the whole person.

If the parable or metaphor connects to the listeners' structures, it can free them to release emotions they may have repressed. It can also help them recognize feelings just outside their awareness. You will see the power of this in the next chapter.

VULNERABILITY

In Chapter One our friend the Acrobat found that, for his students, true freedom was discovering what was inside them and turning it loose. Living behind emotional walls is one of the many ways people remain stuck. When a communicator broadcasts from a place of vulnerability, it invites others to respond from the deeper places inside their own soul.

Vulnerability can shift the atmosphere of a room. While overtly expressed feelings can stir people, the simple posture of vulnerability suggests that more is possible. It sends the message that it is safe to connect to more than specific emotions; it is also safe to "just be yourself."

Vulnerability invites empathy and as researcher Brené Brown says, "Empathy is the antidote to shame."

As school teachers, motivational speakers, preachers, and parents, we all send our messages into the same territory—the human soul. Whether our goal is education, motivation, or liberation, we must figure out how to navigate our listeners' internal interactive system of cognition, beliefs, drives, and emotions. The more we understand this territory, the more effectively we can craft our messages to hit the desired targets.

With that in mind, let's now look at a trusted model of affecting change in the soul.

LOGICAL LEVELS OF CHANGE

When we want to bring change to a person's soul, we must understand the steps people go through to accept or bring about change. The most helpful model of change is the Logical Levels of Change. This model is a foundational construct of NLP and was first introduced in the book, *Changing Belief Systems with NLP* by Robert Dilts.

Take a look at the basic model in Figure 1 below, and then let's work through it together. Here is Dilts' basic model:

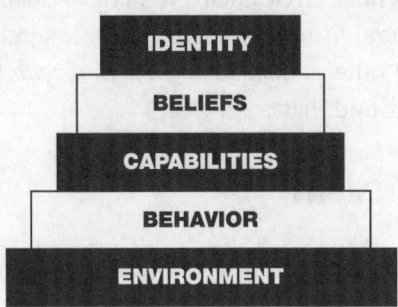

Figure 1

To grasp the helpfulness of this model, I want to build it from the bottom up. When people desire a change of circumstance, status, or relationship, they begin by making changes at the lowest level: *Environment*. As they grow in their understanding of their soul and true personal growth, they begin to look at each successively higher level.

The framework is designed to help us see and think in a hierarchical model of the elements of change. The lowest level, *Environment*, is the least powerful level and the highest level, *Identity*, is the most powerful. That said, I prefer to look at the levels as shown here, in Figure 2:

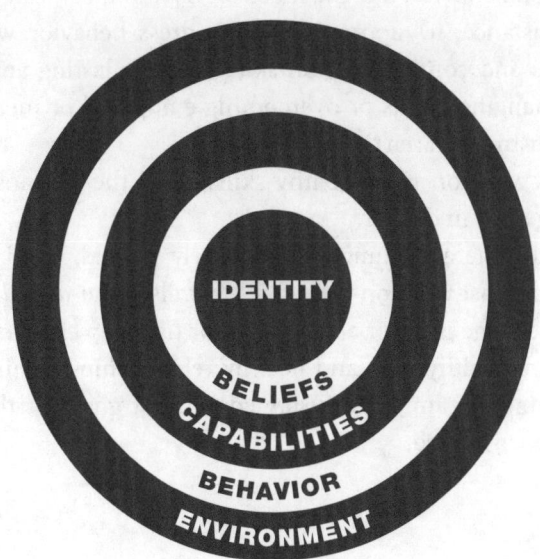

Figure 2

This visual of concentric circles helps to better visualize this model with the teaching in this book. *Identity* is the thing we're aiming to unleash—it's at a person's core, and other constructs—*Beliefs, Capabilities, Behavior* and *Environment*—wrap around that core.

LEVEL 5: ENVIRONMENT

When we seek change, we start at the lowest, or outward level of *Environment*. In our early attempts at change, we frequently look outside ourselves. We wish others would change, or we wish circumstances would change. We focus on others, or we simply decide to change homes, jobs, or spouses. This focus on external change is already a trap because—as we all know—wherever we go, *there we are.*

The hierarchical nature of this model says that if we make changes at one level up, then it will produce automatic change in the level(s) below.

So, at some point in the search for satisfaction, when changing their environment doesn't work, people begin to focus on the next level of change: the level of *Behavior*.

LEVEL 4: BEHAVIOR

This focus on *Behavior*, like the focus on *Environment*, can produce *some* change. For instance, it's appropriate to address behavior when teaching about manners and communication skills. But for lasting and meaningful change, like changing habits or overcoming emotional or mental obstacles, behavioral adjustments aren't enough.

"I need to work on my empathy skills," said the diagnosed narcissist, whose marriage was in danger.

"Indeed!" the therapist quickly and wisely replied. "And, of course, it might help to not just work on your skills, but also your *actual empathy.*"

Behavioral change is never a substitute for the deep changes people need in order to have healthy lives and healthy relationships. While it may be a helpful beginning, it cannot be sustained without going further up in this model…or deeper inward.

LEVEL 3: CAPABILITIES

The challenge is that many people who have attempted change have come to believe they *cannot* succeed. One repeatedly failed effort after another is hard evidence to overcome. This struggle brings us face to face with the barrier that brings many people to a standstill when they try to change—*Capabilities*.

Our limitations function like a thermostat in the soul, a set point, with feedback loops that prevent any meaningful change.

People who can lose ten pounds but not thirty, or people who can change for a week or two but cannot maintain a habit over time, demonstrate the trap of living under a maladjusted thermostat. The thermostat is set, and minimal changes soon meet with strong resistance, making it more and more *and more* difficult to maintain the new habit. Like the heater or air conditioner responding to the thermostat setting in a home, *Capabilities* quickly return people to their status quo.

These *Capabilities*, or thermostat settings, lock us into (or out of) the changes we so desire either in ourselves or in the people we purpose to help. If we could increase our *Capabilities*, we would find new possibilities, but the thermostat in our soul is much harder to adjust than the thermostat on our walls.

To understand the challenge of re-setting our thermostat let's add two new elements to our model—*Thoughts* and *Feelings*:

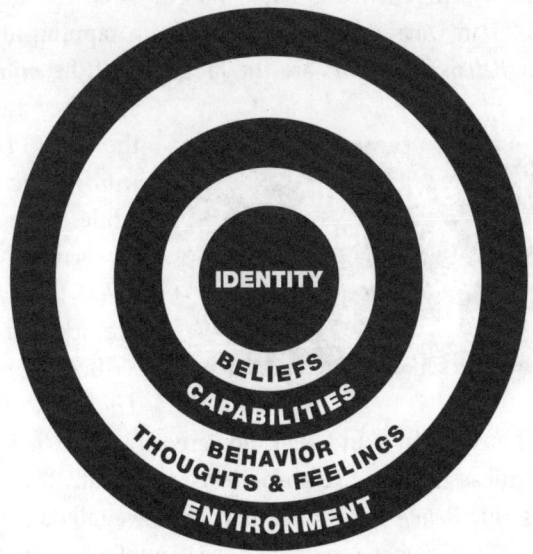

Figure 3

LEVEL 4: REVISITED

Thoughts and *Feelings* are not in the original model, but in my experience, the addition of *Thoughts* and *Feelings* (as included in Figure 3) identify the previous level more in line with our definition of the soul.

Your *Behavior* (your will) is interrelated with your *Thoughts* (your mind) and your *Feelings* (your emotions). Negative *Thoughts* can lead to negative *Feelings* in the same way that negative *Feelings* can feed negative *Thoughts*. Both affect *Behavior*, and both are affected by *Behavior*.

Too often we try to "fake it 'til we make it," using *Thoughts* to change *Feelings*, or *Behavior* to change *Thoughts*. In simple issues, this can work, but in cases of difficult change, these kinds of attempts become like trying to arm-wrestle yourself... where winning and losing happen simultaneously

People stuck in cycles of destructive *Behavior*, *Thoughts*, or *Feelings* often try to change by operating only at the level of *Capability*. But temporary "victory" is no victory at all—because every time the cycle repeats, another mountain of evidence "proves" that meaningful change is impossible. It is an on again/off again type of change that only fosters growing frustration.

How then do we change the thermostat? What settings are possible? We change it by *resetting* it...by changing our *Beliefs*.

LEVEL 2: BELIEFS

Beliefs are quite different from *Thoughts* but often the words are used interchangeably or in ways that can keep us from tapping into the power of changing our *Beliefs*. *Thoughts* are the language of the *mind*, but *Beliefs* are the atmosphere of the *heart*. *Thoughts* have *words* attached to them, while some of our most powerful and impacting *Beliefs* took root *before* we ever learned to speak.

> "THOUGHTS ARE THE LANGUAGE OF THE MIND, BUT BELIEFS ARE THE ATMOSPHERE OF THE HEART."

Because of this, our *Thoughts*, *Feelings*, and *Behaviors* are all steered by—and even powered by—our *Beliefs*. *Beliefs* are those very core ideas that we are absolutely certain of. Reality doesn't inform our minds; our *Beliefs* do. Remember when we talked about Structure in Chapter Two? That's what our *Beliefs* are—our Structures. The two are synonymous.

The kind of *Beliefs* referred to here are core *Beliefs* that are deep and enduring. They include things like:

- "Am I valuable?"

- "Am I safe?"

- "What makes me valuable?"

- "Is God safe?"

These core *Beliefs* are shaped early in life and are often not in our conscious minds until something brings them to our consciousness. This is important to note because bringing these unconscious structures into the conscious mind is an important part of helping people reset their thermostats.

Beliefs are the gateway to the release of *Identity*. Healthy *Beliefs* release it. Unhealthy or inaccurate *Beliefs* imprison it.

LEVEL 1: IDENTITY

Meaningful change ultimately happens when people unleash their true *Identity*. That release is what people identify as freedom. If attempts to help people change move them toward any goal that is not in line with their true Identity, those attempts are unlikely to succeed and, in many ways, can be harmful.

Remember, the *Identity* is a pre-determined or pre-existing structure that is either *restrained* or *released* by the *Belief* system. All attempts to help people move toward meaningful change need to be tied back to *Identity* and therefore must target changing *Beliefs* more than *Thoughts*.

Remember Jane from Chapter Two? She had tried to change her *Behavior*. Her *Behavior* and *Thoughts* concerning relationships were subject to Structures or Beliefs that no thought or action seemed able to change. Her capabilities failed her; her thermostat needed to be reset.

At the same time she listened to ideas about success, she also received the constant, non-verbal message that she was failing. While she fed her positive *Thoughts*, her negative *Beliefs* were still validated. In the end, positive *Thoughts* didn't win out; her *Beliefs* of shame and failure drove her. That's why many well-meaning speakers did her more harm than good.

This much is clear: Deep, lasting and meaningful change does not come from teaching information or urging willpower. Words alone are insufficient to reach the *Belief* level. *Deep, lasting and meaningful change comes from impacting a* Belief. When people see themselves in new ways, they will experience themselves in new ways. When people see God in a new way, they will respond to Him in a new way. Give someone a new thought and it is subject to the thermostat of *Capabilities*. Open their eyes to a new way of seeing or thinking, and the thermostat is reset.

Dilts' Logical Levels of Change model then gives us a target: Change people's beliefs and they will change their own lives.

"HELP ME HELP YOU...HELP YOU"

Watch what happens when a human soul is returned to its original design. Far too often we try to bring about change by targeting the level of *Behavior*, maybe because we believe that the problem Jesus came to solve is the problem of human behavior. In reality, what Jesus came to "fix"—the thing that changed in the Garden of Eden—was our *Identity*.

What changed at that level was that man, who was once filled with the Breath of Life, was now filled with death. He had lost that connection and left the Garden. Once man's *Identity* was devoid of life, his *Belief* system went into action to manufacture an acceptable alternative to the feeling of being dead. Performance… compulsiveness…any counterfeit would do.

Doesn't that force you to think differently about this thing we call sin— what Jesus *died* for? Sin is much less a negative *Behavior* and much more the condition of an empty soul.

This also puts Jesus' death and resurrection in a new light. His death is more than simply a legal payment for our misbehavior. It is an exchange of His death for ours, and our life for His. What He offered us was not a new set of expectations but rather a new "self," a new *Identity*. Whereas our old self was inherited from Adam and Eve, our new selves are generated by the power of Jesus' resurrection.

The most powerful change we can help people make is to help them find and then release their new self, restored by Jesus' invitation.

Words like "salvation" (re-establishing our intended *Identity* through connection to God) and "sanctification" (discovering and uncovering this new self) have lost their ability to point people to such a transformational thought process. Or perhaps we have lost our ability to hear the true meaning of these words. Either way, to find these truths powerful again, we must hear them in a new way.

A new thought process, which is actually another biblical word that we have drained of its potency—"repentance"—can allow us to access ancient and powerful truth. We must offer more than knowledge and help people change their *Beliefs* so their new man can be released.

CHANGING OUR COMMUNICATION

Based on this model, the communication strategies in this book have two important functions. The first is to change our objective from targeting *Behavior*, *Thoughts*, and *Feelings*, to targeting *Beliefs*. When we learn how to help people change a *Belief*, the other important changes are a natural result.

The second function of our communication strategies is to encourage us to reach inside the circles to make a connection with the person inside (his or her *Identity*) and invite that person to come out and play. Communication that helps facilitate change reaches from our soul to the soul of another and welcomes that person to become himself or herself in our presence.

Imagine if a well-meaning person set out to help our friend Jane. If he delivered genuinely helpful information that reached her mind but delivered it in such a way that she felt shamed or belittled. Her beliefs and therefore her behaviors thoughts and feelings would be shaped more by his delivery than by his words. This is why in Chapter Two I say the "way" always matters more than the "what."

With this roadmap for transformation at our fingertips, let's now switch our focus and look at the other side of the brain—the right side—that so deeply allows us to bypass the soul and reach right into people's deepest selves.

STUDY GUIDE

KEY CONCEPTS

- The human soul is composed of the mind, the will, and the emotions.

- The will is most powerful when it feels free to choose.

- Emotions are drivers.

- *Beliefs* have power over *Behavior*, *Thoughts*, and *Feelings*.

- Jesus didn't just die for what you have done; He died for who you are.

SKILL BUILDERS

1. Ask yourself: *Am I valuable? What about me gives me value?*

2. Learn about the will: Some people more naturally resist input, others more naturally comply. Watch people this week to see if you can tell their style.

3. Think of a time that you had a *Belief* shift—when your picture of you changed, or your picture of something important changed. What changed this belief?

4. As you listen to others, see if you can identify beliefs that they have just by listening to their language.

CHAPTER 7

HOW CONNECTION UNLEASHES POWER

The riddles of God are more satisfying than the solutions of man.
—G. K. Chesterton

Art is not a thing, it is a way.
—Elbert Hubbard

Ahh, the right brain. The creative one. The one that makes up bedtime stories—and the one few speakers use to its fullest potential. In Chapter Four, we focused on the left brain and the power of words to lock or unlock the mind. Now, we will explore the benefits and methodology of teaching to the right brain which uses parable, emotion, and creativity. One is not better than the other. In an ideal world, the left and right brain function in perfect balance. However, depending on the audience and the setting, one might be a more effective choice for enabling change in our listeners. In honor of this hemisphere of the brain, let me tell you three stories about a story.

STORY #1: STIRRED BY THE TRUTH

He had sat on the aisle about three rows back, looking proper in his suit. Like the other students, he had kept his eyes focused on me the entire time but seemed no more or less responsive than anyone else in class.

At the end of our session, he approached me with his facial expression still flat, but he pointed at his cheeks. Specifically, he was pointing at the liquid flowing down his seemingly unaffected cheeks.

"What are these?" he asked forcefully and uncertain. "What are these, and why are they coming out of my eyes?"

I looked back at him surprised both at the strange evidence of emotion from his eyes and his apparent surprise at that emotion. My mind caught up to the moment, and I asked him if he planned to be back the following week. He assured me he did.

> **"IS IT BETTER FOR A TEACHER TO HELP STUDENTS EXPERIENCE BUT NOT UNDERSTAND—OR TO UNDERSTAND BUT NOT EXPERIENCE?"**

"Great!" I said. "This week's class was entirely right-brained. You experienced it but did not understand it. Next week I will explain to your left brain what your right brain heard today."

This was a common experience that people had when listening to Jesus' teaching—and I felt honored to have the same response! That student had felt something change inside him, but he had no cognitive understanding of what that change was. In other words, he experienced something he simply could not understand.

This begs an important question: Is it better for a teacher to help students experience but not understand—or to understand but not experience?

The man had sat through a class with no teaching. He had simply listened to me tell the Parable of the Acrobat. While everyone understood the story, somewhere inside each of them, they were stirred by the truth *under* the story. This man's left brain had heard a story about an acrobat. His right brain had connected with something more…something hidden in his heart. And the effect was deeply moving.

THE POWER OF STORY

In Chapter One, I continued a story—a parable—that I began in my first book, *Think Differently Live Differently.* The first part of the story opens with the story of a newborn acrobat who is lost on a path, found, and raised by farmers. The story reaches key structures that are universal to the human experience. (You can read the full parable at the beginning of my book, *Think Differently Live Differently,* or watch me teaching it online at vimeo. com/30750987.)

I wrote the story to help listeners connect with something greater than themselves, something born into them—and in all of us—from the beginning of time. It connects with the great disappointment of loss, of hope, and of the expectation that something in us was meant for greatness. It connects with our hunger for redemption and our struggle to live as someone made for greatness…even if all we experience is smallness.

The story takes us from the unrestrained joy of the Garden to the Fall, from the despair of the Fall to Redemption, from the mystery of Redemption to Restoration, and from the process of Restoration to a life of Freedom. These structures are ours because every individual, regardless of culture or time, are created in the image of God and in the Story of God. The goal of the story is to help people think differently about their lives and their journeys to freedom.

The man who met me with tears in his eyes after hearing the Parable of the Acrobat learned something with his right brain that his left brain didn't know he was learning. He experienced it but did not understand it.

JESUS, WHY DO YOU TEACH LIKE THAT?

The issue of Jesus' teachings and His teaching style was never more on display than when He finished teaching the Parable of the Sower, sometimes known as the Parable of the Soils. This is one of His more complex parables with several moving parts and a range of ideas and images. It is one of only a few of His parables that He explained. It is also the only time recorded where His disciples questioned His teaching style.

Were they genuinely curious about why Jesus chose this method of teaching? I don't believe so. Instead, I submit that they were trying to help Jesus be a better Messiah. It's as if they thought His teaching style needed help being more relevant and socially acceptable. And when they questioned Him on it, they gave Jesus one more opportunity to shift their brains. Let me share with you how I interpret—and paraphrase—this conversation.

> *"Master," they inquired, "why do you teach in parables?"*
>
> *"I teach in parables," He responded, "so that the people will not learn what I am teaching."*
>
> *They exchange confused looks and the sideways glances as if to say, "He's doing that thing again. I told you it was a bad idea to question Him."*

What kind of teacher, what kind of lesson, has as a primary strategy that the students *will not learn*? Let's consider some issues concerning brain development as we allow this concept to change our communication styles.

CONNECTION AND LABELS

A few years back, I attended a breakout session at a counselor's conference. A counselor named Pamela Bermender taught a session about neuroscience and attachment in couples counseling. Exciting, right!? I could hardly wait!

She did a whole session, but the very first element set my thoughts on fire. In fact, it is one of the reasons this book exists. Here is what she said:

In the first 18-24 months of life, the primary development of the brain takes place in the right hemisphere. During those crucial months, the infant develops one thing: *Attachment*. The infant connects deeply to his or her caretakers. With no language and no ability to learn (at least not in the way we think about learning), the child simply *connects*. The right brain grows in response to connection. It doesn't store data; it processes *experience*.

As an infant connects to his or her caretakers, the right hemisphere of the brain develops, and its development is all about the experience and awareness of relationships. The child's brain puts no organization on what it's receiving. What it does have is a rich, profound experience of connecting.

Deep eye contact and all the developing facial expressions demonstrate the child is processing attachment and the emotional experiences of relatedness. The right brain is the center of attachment. The lack of organizational left-brain activity in no way diminishes this experience and, in fact, we see that connection might actually be enhanced in the absence of language.

Somewhere during that time, the left brain fires up and the child begins to attach labels to those experiences. Remember how words are symbols? The first time the baby utters the syllable "ma" and the mother responds with excitement, the child begins to attach the label "ma" to the experience of being mothered and the person who mothers him or her.

Bit by bit, syllable by syllable, the child begins to attach labels to the experiences and connections he or she has accrued over those first months. The left hemisphere begins to develop as language develops. Now that deep inner experience has a label, or a name, and the left hemisphere can begin to analyze and organize the outside world according to these labels.

The development of the brain begins a migration from the right hemisphere and attachment to the left hemisphere and the development of language and analysis. This migration continues as the complexity of language and organization grows.

The hairy one responds to "dada." The smooth one responds to "mama." The hairy one and the smooth one seem to go together more often than not. One of those "parental units" seems easier to persuade than the other. *One feeds me more. One plays with me more.*

All this organization utilizes the newly acquired labels. Perhaps all this is so that one day the child can tell a therapist which parent he or she has issues with. Whatever the reason the right and left hemisphere develop what is intended to be an amazing partnership!

The right brain can experience connection but not describe it, while the left brain can describe relationships and connections but not experience them. As long as both hemispheres function in concert, the child can grow both to describe *and* experience people, life, and attachments.

Neither is designed to operate without the other, but either one can operate independently. In the migration of brain development, the right brain was never meant to be left out of the process. But we all know it is possible to develop language for concepts we do not actually experience. We function too much from knowledge and develop the ability to "know something in our head" but struggle to "know it in our hearts." If we have experiences that are deep and profound, we may struggle to put them into language and end up simply saying things like, "It's hard to explain, you just had to have been there."

One way of knowing produces experience without labels, and the other way of knowing produces language without experience. As a teacher, if I had to aim for one, I would aim for experience without knowledge far more than knowledge without experience, but all teachers must decide that for themselves.

STORY #2: TRANSMITTING GOD'S POWER

My first time to ever speak through an interpreter was in Haifa, Israel. The congregation was made up primarily of Russian-speaking Jews. Never having spoken through translation before, and with only one opportunity to share, I wanted to leave them with something meaningful.

I struggled with how to do this in a single setting with all the obstacles of culture and language. The Lord didn't seem to struggle as much as I did. When I asked Him how I should approach the situation, I felt His answer was to simply use the evening to tell them a parable. So once again, I began to tell the Parable of the Acrobat.

My translator was a Russian woman named Helga. Helga was prepared to assist me, but neither of us were prepared for what happened that night. I began to tell the story phrase by phrase, and Helga began to translate it. Suddenly, one of the phrases connected unexpectedly to a structure deep in Helga's soul. As I spoke a single phrase in English, the meaning of the story hit her. She opened her mouth, but the only sounds that came out were guttural cries. She cried so deeply she had to walk off the stage.

Picture this from the perspective of the Russians sitting in the congregation. Their beloved friend Helga was doing her job one minute, and the next she left the stage in tears. *The American must have said something to send her sobbing from the platform!* I stood there watching them watch me. All we heard was Helga crying softly from the nearby room.

By the time Helga came back, they were on the edge of their seats eager to find out what had happened. More importantly, Helga had connected to the story, and in doing so, she had connected to God. For the rest of the night, Helga broadcast something that was coming from a place inside her that was freshly opened and freshly healed. She translated my story, but more importantly, she transferred her healing to the crowd as she spoke.

Her method was powerfully congruent with her message. She was lost, then found, and then transformed. What had once seemed like an obstacle— working through translation—became the very mechanism of transmitting God's power that night.

CONNECTING THROUGH PARABLES

Now, let's return to Jesus teaching His disciples. They had just asked Him the question, "Why do you teach in parables?" and as I paraphrased earlier,

Jesus answered, "I teach in parables so that you will *not learn* what I am teaching you."

If I could paraphrase one last time with the "*Hamplified Version*" of the Bible, I would say that He said, "I teach in parables, so you will not learn with your left brain what I want you to learn with your right brain. I teach in parables so that you will not believe that your way of learning has or is even able to produce the result I am after."

Jesus refused to cater to a method of learning that produced words without power and was deeply committed to a method of teaching and learning that connected people to their Father.

Let's move beyond my paraphrase to hear what Jesus actually said to His helpful disciples. Here was His answer:

> "*Because you have been given the chance to understand the secrets of the kingdom of Heaven," replied Jesus, "but they have not. For when a man has something, more is given to him till he has plenty. But if he has nothing even his nothing will be taken away from him. This is why I speak to them in these parables; because they go through life with their eyes open, but see nothing, and with their ears open, but understand nothing of what they hear. They are the living fulfilment of Isaiah's prophecy which says: 'Hearing you will hear and shall not understand, and seeing you will see and not perceive; for the heart of this people has grown dull. Their ears are hard of hearing and their eyes they have closed, lest they should see with their eyes and hear with their ears, lest they should understand with their heart and turn, so that I should heal them.'*" –Matthew 13:11-15, PHILLIPS

In other words, Jesus said, "I teach in parables because people have learned to hear in a way that doesn't allow them to experience what I am saying. I teach in such a way that is designed to shift the way they hear. If they hear in the same way I am teaching, they could turn and be healed."

Jesus proclaimed this another way two chapters earlier: "At that time Jesus said, 'I praise You, Father, Lord of heaven and earth, that You have hidden these things from the wise and intelligent and have revealed them to infants'" (Matthew 11:25).

Here we see the strategy. God has hidden the kind of truth He wants to communicate from those who only think with their left brain and made it plain to those who think with their right.

What if the mysteries of the kingdom are more about connecting to the Father than they are about comprehending ideas and analysis about Him?

What if Jesus refuses to feed the mind that expects information because He knows most minds will stop there and never proceed back to attachment?

Much like a newborn connecting with her earthly parents (right brain) before she develops language (left brain), the mysteries hidden in parables are more about connecting to and experiencing God than they are about *understanding* (or at least our definition of understanding).

If we erect the idol of comprehending labels and organized ideas, we will raise it like a golden calf and worship our idea of God as if it is actually God. As long as we live in the mystery of hard-to-label experience, we can know God, rather than only know *about* God. As soon as we begin to know *about* Him, we let our own knowledge be our source of comfort instead of receiving from the One we know.

Somewhere in the transition, where learning moves from the right-brain experience of connection and attachment to the left-brain process of labeling and organizing, the concept of "learning" begins to shift.

As "thinking" crosses over the corpus callosum, the part of the brain that joins the two hemispheres, it is possible to move past the beautiful equilibrium between experience *and* label. When we do, people begin to "know a lot of things in their heads that they struggle to know in their hearts."

In many ways, this process of moving from the right brain to the left brain can be compared to the move from the Tree of Life to the Tree of the Knowledge of Good and Evil. The Tree of Life is filled with power and experience while the other is only filled with information.

THE MESSAGE OF THE MANNA

Consider God's motivation for giving the Israelites manna while they wandered in the wilderness. In Exodus 16:4, God said He would give the Israelites manna in the desert with the instruction to collect only enough for each day. His reason was to test them to see if they would obey.

Pick enough for the day, you will eat that day. Pick enough for two days, the excess will rot. God's provision was available within God's guidelines. But what was He saying? What was the message of the manna?

In Hebrew, the word "manna" is actually a question that means, "What is it?" The Israelites walked out on day one, saw a strange substance on the ground, and asked, "What is it?"

The implicit answer was, "I don't know, but pick it up, and you will eat today."

But the deeper answer was also hidden in the question. If manna is known by the label "What is it?" then as soon as they knew "what it was," it ceased to be manna. As soon as it became knowledge, it was no longer life sustaining food.

> **"JESUS' TEACHING WAS MANNA IN THE DESERT OF HUMAN UNDERSTANDING."**

Did you catch that? When our learning is defined as learning labels, it is no longer a life-sustaining connection, and we come up after a class and ask, "What are these?" while pointing to our tear-soaked eyes.

Jesus' teaching was manna in the desert of human understanding. While the left brain asks, "What is it?", the right brain feasts on the mystery of a Father who wants to attach to His children.

Left-brain versus right-brain thinking is more than just concrete versus abstract thinking. It is also knowledge versus experience and information versus attachment.

If this is the case, people who teach and communicate through primarily left-brained approaches (like content delivery and educational approaches) would unwittingly create pseudo-disciples who understand with their minds but cannot understand with their hearts. They might have a form of godliness but lack the power that comes from being attached to God.

And if that is the case, it is imperative that we who want to bring meaningful change into people's lives develop a significant understanding of right-brained approaches to communication.

STORY #3: "WELCOME HOME!"

My friend Alan and I had shown up at an undisclosed location in Asia with plans to teach a full week on the topic our hosts had requested. Over our first meal, we were thrilled to hear our hosts say that they had previewed our material. Then the leader told us he wanted us to change course.

Rather than teach 40 hours on our intended topic, he instead asked if we could teach for 40 hours on the Kingdom of God. With no preparation and having only brought notes and presentations for a different topic, we made a quick turn and spent the next 40 hours watching amazing things happen.

I had no way of knowing what would happen on day three. And, yes, it involved a certain parable about a certain acrobat.

Set in a Western-style hotel, the meeting included a group of men and women who served as pastors and leaders in risky parts of the world. Some of them had been arrested, and at least one had been tortured for his faith. Once again, I wondered what I could share with people who had served at that level.

We were improvising that week. My friend Alan and I had to take stock every few hours and ask the Lord and each other what to do next. Midway through the week, we felt it was the time to tell the Parable of the Acrobat.

Our translator was a young Chinese man who had served faithfully and energetically all week. I found myself again in the familiar seesaw rhythm of speaking through a translator. As far as I knew, the translator was doing a great job.

Then without warning, everything changed.

In the story, the acrobat returns home to his birth parents and to the life he was born to have to become the person he was born to be. Transformational moments arise between the acrobat and his birth parents and a key moment occurs when he is convinced that he is failing at stepping into his identity as an acrobat.

In an emotional exchange between him and his birth father, the young man expresses his fear of letting his father down. The father responds with the simple words, "If you never perform on the trapeze or high wire, our lives are already complete. We don't need you to perform. We thought you were lost forever. Now, you are home with us. This is all we have ever wanted. We don't need you to perform. We are simply glad you are home."

The translator uttered these last words, and suddenly, a strange sound came from the back of the room. It was a cross between a grunt and a sob, like someone had been punched in the gut. The grunt was followed by deep sobs, and then another grunt came from somewhere else in the room.

Sounds of crying filled the room, but something more happened. The room felt thick, the air heavier. God was doing something, and He hadn't asked our permission.

Soon most of the men and women in the room sobbed deep, gut-wrenching sobs. Many lay on the floor or curled into a fetal position in their seats.

I stopped speaking and stood transfixed alongside the translator and the leader of this network, unsure of my next step.

The leader took my microphone and began to repeat a simple phrase in Chinese. Softly into the microphone, he said the same thing over and over.

He turned to Alan and me and told us to go lay hands on these men and women and pray from our spirits.

He continued to pray one thing over and over.

Our left brains had no idea what was happening, but without a doubt, these men and women were experiencing some kind of connection that none of us could explain or comprehend.

Later we put together what had happened. These leaders had been raised in a culture where dictatorship was their leadership paradigm. They had served God faithfully—even being thrown into prison because they saw Him as the best dictator they could serve. But none of them had a paradigm for a God who wanted to father sons and daughters.

Their heavenly Father gave them a new paradigm. He did not do it by explaining Fatherhood, He did it by Fathering the little orphans in their souls. In a moment, He had torn down the structure of God as dictator and replaced it by sending the Spirit of adoption, causing their hearts to cry, "Daddy!" He changed their beliefs, and in doing so, unlocked their identities.

I didn't make it happen.

I didn't know it was even an option!

My part was simple. I refused to teach their left brain. I refused to stimulate the part of their minds that learned ideas. More importantly, I simply offered an opportunity to bypass their defenses and their logical thoughts and hear God say a simple phrase to them over and over again.

We asked the leader what he had been praying as he prayed the one phrase over and over again.

"What was I praying?" he responded, "I was simply praying, 'Welcome home.'"

For the rest of our lives, we can teach the theology of a home with God in heaven. Or we can tell little boys and girls who are starved for connection to their Father, "Welcome home." These men and women were lost and then found, and then they were home.

8 WAYS TO TARGET THE RIGHT BRAIN

If change is your goal as a communicator, this is one important shift—the most important. Providing information to people simply spurs more left-brain development and can actually move people away from change. If you want to reach the hearts of people and the structures by which they grow and change, target the right hemisphere of the brain.

Parables are not the only way to do this. Keep in mind the right side of

121

the brain is about connection. Here are some ways to reach the right side of the brain:

1. **Connect to Your Listeners:** Use their names, look them in the eyes, and ask them questions that pull them into a two-way engagement.

2. **Tell Personal Stories:** Stories make a place for common ground and common ground makes a place for connection.

3. **Use Diagrams or Other Visual Methods:** Allow the visual part of the mind to see some of the structures or ideas you are communicating.

4. **Be Vulnerable:** Open your heart as you speak or write. Share *you*. Your vulnerability is the first half of connection

5. **Learn to Improvise (See Chapter 10):** Improvisation is a right-brained approach. Right brain speaks to right brain.

6. **Use Pictures:** Show your listeners beauty, show them connections, show them babies and puppies. Do this not to manipulate, but to invite them to experience rather than catalogue.

7. **Pause:** Watch your listeners. Give them silent time to process. While you may not have a dialogue in a large group setting, if your listeners are processing, give them time to do so. This is the verbal equivalent of a *selah,* or pause, to allow things to sink in. Pay attention to your listeners and learn to read them well.

8. **Listen for God's Direction:** When you speak *from* connection, you increase the likelihood that you will lead your listeners *into* connection.

Information matters. Information or ideas comprise one of the building blocks of communication. Keep in mind that just because you have delivered the building materials, your listeners do not yet have a house. Give them the information they need to build with, but then be sure that you help them build through right-brain techniques. Without a house, you can never welcome them home.

TWO WAYS TO TEACH: LEFT VS. RIGHT BRAIN TEACHING

Clearly, not only do the left and right brain receive differently, but as teachers, we can target them differently. That's the reason I began this book with a parable, but then have also provided key concepts to reach the left-brain.

This reminds me of a time when I had an assignment to write a post for a co-op blog written mostly by women for women. I wanted to write about how strongholds—destructive and repetitive thought patterns—develop. As I looked over what I wrote, I thought that the information was clear and accurate, but I didn't like it. I felt my readers would likely find the piece not very engaging.

> **"WHEN YOU SPEAK FROM CONNECTION, YOU INCREASE THE LIKELIHOOD THAT YOU WILL LEAD YOUR LISTENERS INTO CONNECTION."**

It struck me that it might be helpful to write the same ideas from a completely different angle. What follows are both writings—one engages the left brain, the other the right brain. They are an example of the difference between the two hemispheres. Read them with the mind of a teacher, examining not only the content but also the process of communication. Also pay attention to the impact of the two styles on your own experience.

METHOD NUMBER ONE: TARGETING THE LEFT BRAIN

Anatomy of a Stronghold

Second Corinthians 10:3-5 states, "For though we walk in the flesh, we do not war according to the flesh, for the weapons of our warfare are not of the flesh, but divinely powerful for the destruction of fortresses (strongholds). We are destroying speculations and every lofty thing raised up against the knowledge of God, and we are taking every thought captive to the obedience of Christ."

The author specifically tells us we are pulling down strongholds, or a structure of thought(s) built on a cycle involving experiences, thoughts, and internal responses to those thoughts. These thoughts and internal responses then shape our external relationships. In many cases, because our external relationships are organized by the lies and internal responses, they can actually replicate the very experiences that caused the cycle in the first place.

Our lives provide a range of experiences. Often in the more painful experiences, we may hear deceptive thoughts or lies in our minds. These lies are most often about God, ourselves, or the nature of reality.

As those lies run through our thoughts, the more painful or confusing they are, the more we are prone to make conscious or unconscious decisions to respond to our pain or discomfort. It is these choices that begin to shape our souls. When we try to protect ourselves from future pain, or comfort ourselves in present pain, we not only become self-protective, but we also begin to build an external version of ourselves based on protection instead of our identity.

This false self becomes the version of ourselves that we present to the world. As we live from this false or protected self, we begin to form our relationships out of and in response to our false self.

This network of relationships built around our false self and in response to painful experiences has a great likelihood of repeating the very experiences that motivated their formation in the first place. This completes a cycle that can and often does repeat itself throughout our lifetime, and this completes the formation of a stronghold.

We tear it down not simply by correcting our information and improving our methods of self-protection. We tear it down by changing from self as source to *God* as source.

As we allow God to replace the lies we believe with His truth, and we surrender our self-protection to His protection, the cycle is reversed, and the stronghold can be torn down.

METHOD NUMBER TWO: TARGETING THE RIGHT BRAIN

Somewhere Inside You Lives YOU

Somewhere inside you, *you* live—the beautiful one who is unafraid and unashamed. Somewhere inside you, *you* sing. Or scream. Or whisper. You may be forgotten, but you, yourself, have not forgotten. Silenced perhaps. Hidden away beneath layers of life and circumstance, but you are in there somewhere.

The war against you has been unrelenting, sometimes vicious, sometimes subtle. Either way, vicious or subtle, the war is always to steal from you all that you were created to be. The war tests you and surprises you. If the battle can convince you to hide, to run, or to self-protect, the tide turns against you. Hard on the outside, a false front, you run from the battle.

You ask yourself, "How could they say that? How could they do that? How could they not see the tear rolling down my cheek?"

The war rages all around and tries to steal from you all that you were made to be. Year after year after year after year, you hide. How can you keep the pain from soaking in? You become strong...or do you? You learn how to be smarter than the others. You learn how to be harder than the others. You learn all the ways to be stronger than anyone else in the battle. Your brain. Your body. What to do, what not to do—all carefully calculated to provide a safe passage through.

Or, is it the death of you?

When you were little, you danced and played when no one knew. You sang when it was in your heart. You looked joyfully at your big eyes in the mirror and had yet to hear the voice of self-criticism. You danced and played again. When you were little, you cried unashamedly and laughed till you snorted. This made you laugh more, even when someone heard you. When you were little, you had yet to be betrayed and had yet to betray yourself. When you were little, *you lived.*

The war against you has taken its toll. You are too tired to dance and play. Or too ashamed. It is hard to tell the difference. You now need to be protected *from* the ways you have protected yourself. Your walls keep others out, but they also keep you *in*. Locked tightly behind your own clever strategies, you hide.

You hide from them, and you hide from yourself. You hide so well, you cannot find yourself.

But somewhere inside you, *you* live—the beautiful one who is unafraid and unashamed. You sing, still, whether you listen or not. You cry, whether you listen or not.

Somewhere inside you, you live. Hidden away beneath layers of life and circumstances, you hope that you will care for "the you" inside like the others did not. You hope you will introduce "the you" inside to the One who made you. You hope you will be the one who takes care of you. You hope you will hear your song and invite yourself to dance and play again. You hope you will no longer join the war against yourself. You hope you can discover what you need and help yourself find it. You hope you will pull down the walls and introduce yourself to the One who made you. You hope you will play, you hope that you will let yourself tell you who you are.

Somewhere inside you, you live. Come out and play.

COMPARE AND CONTRAST

Let's examine these two methods. Clearly, the first was designed to be a heavily left-brained, academic approach. The second was a very right-brained, creative approach. Neither of these is right or wrong. Instead, this exercise is to demonstrate how each of the brain's hemispheres can and should influence both expressive and receptive communication. If you are teaching this to a room full of engineers, the first approach might be the most effective. If you are teaching a room full of artists or writers, the second might be the most effective. You can also switch it up and challenge each group to a brand-new way of thinking.

Most importantly, if your goal is to change your listeners, you should intentionally choose a method that can both meet them where they are and also shift them to a new way of learning.

The first method is a fairly plain presentation of information. The address to the reader uses the pronouns we, us, and our but does not develop a real connection to the readers.

The second is an entirely different approach to the same ideas. This comparison is helpful and allows people to recognize that ideas exist hidden behind the curtain of words and words have infinite ways to express ideas. It is not simply about abstraction; it is about connection.

What makes the second method such a right-brained approach is that it is almost entirely descriptive of experience and not of cognition. For those who are familiar with this experience, it can be like hearing an old song that they haven't heard in a long time. If that song was meaningful in some way, the song isn't only pleasant, but it also accesses all the meaning and experience of the period in life when the song was so meaningful.

The second method intentionally bypasses cognition and targets the "old songs" that are familiar to people who feel trapped inside themselves. This internal echo reaches and teaches a part of them that is not trying to learn, but instead finds itself gently urged into a new way of engaging.

I would still call this learning, but it is not at all the classic Western method of learning. The Western approach views the mind as something to be filled. The Eastern style of learning considers the soul as a roadmap to be entered and traveled. Turn now and let's view that roadmap together.

Are you ready to pull out your maps to learn new roads to start exploring?

Good! Let's roll down the windows, turn on some music, and go!

STUDY GUIDE

KEY CONCEPTS

- The right brain experiences things it cannot explain. The left brain can explain things it cannot experience.

- The right brain is about attachment.

- The Western mind desires the left-brained approach, but it needs the right-brained approach.

- Parables engage the right hemisphere of the brain.

SKILL BUILDERS

1. Try to say the same thing two different ways. The first time, use direct language. The second time, use metaphor or parable.

2. Develop a parable to help people understand an important time in your life.

3. This week look people in the eye more directly and a bit longer when you speak to them. Notice how it is different for you and for others.

CHAPTER 8

TEACHING FROM THE SPIRIT

We are spirits in the material world.
—The Police, *Spirits in the Material World*

I am not a teacher, but an awakener.
—Robert Frost

It was late in the evening, and it was hot in the second-floor gathering place. Soft crying came from several of the clusters of men and women still standing and praying for each other. Russian interspersed with Hebrew and English floated in the air as did a thick sense of God's presence.

Helga, my translator from Chapter Seven, had done a powerful job of broadcasting God's healing work in her that night. Almost every one of the Russian-speaking people had risen from their seats to receive prayer. Freedom was the target, and they all seemed hungry, eager to respond to whatever was happening.

The dilemma? None of them spoke English, and none of us spoke Russian. We had eight people on our team and four translators. Almost 100 people came for prayer. A translator stood by my side as the evening unfolded. I saw beautiful release and joy on the faces of men and women who came down carrying heavy burdens and asking for relief from the weight of their pasts.

In the back and forth of translated words, the faces communicated the most. Faces, contorted from exhaustion and anguish, shifted to relief and joy as those hungry believers came to ask God for help. The language seemed secondary to the invisible exchange that happened in almost every encounter.

As I finished praying with the last of them, I caught my breath and looked around. One of my friends, equally tired and refreshed, approached me. His eyes wide, he began to tell me about his experiences. He had no translator, but men and women had come to him anyway. In Russian, they had poured out to him with distraught faces and voices.

With no cognitive understanding, he had listened and then prayed whatever he felt God was saying to him. He had prayed in English. They had listened in Russian. He had witnessed the same powerful transformation that I had. Clearly, language and human comprehension were the least important parts of the exchange that took place that night.

WHAT IS "SPIRITUAL"?

> It is these things that we talk about, not using the expressions of the human intellect but those which the Holy Spirit teaches us, explaining things to those who are spiritual. But the unspiritual man simply cannot accept the matters which the Spirit deals with—they just don't make sense to him, for, after all, you must be spiritual to see spiritual things. The spiritual man, on the other hand, has an insight into the meaning of everything, though his insight may baffle the man of the world. This is because the former is sharing in God's wisdom, and 'Who has known the mind of the Lord that he may instruct him?' Incredible as it may sound, we who are spiritual have the very thoughts of Christ!
> —1 Corinthians 2:13-16, PHILLIPS

God has uniquely designed and created humankind. No other being came into existence through this process of blending together the physicality of the Earth and the breath of God.

With this one-of-a-kind makeup of spirit, soul, and body, man has a unique assignment. God created us to stand with one foot in the spiritual realm and one foot in the material realm and pull the two realms together through his way of living and being. I call this "taking dominion over the creation."

Part of our task is to learn what kind of "living and being" pulls these two worlds together. Discovering what kind of *learning* pulls these two worlds together is the assignment of this book. And according to the passage above, spiritual things can only be appraised by or through our spiritual nature.

If this is the case, we should consider what that means. If the construct of the human being is spirit, soul, and body, perhaps the least understood yet most important of these elements is *the spirit*. Far too often, we describe living by the spirit—the transformation and maturation process of spiritual men and women—in behavioral terms. Doing so leads us to misconstrue that spiritual maturity is *attained* by behavior instead of *recognized* by behavior.

For all of our talk of words, symbols,and meaning, one of the most confusing words for people to process is the word "spirit," or even worse, "spiritual." These words have suffered so many attachments over the years that they connect to something different for almost every listener.

The language around spirituality and religious communities often decays because this type of language refers to abstract or ethereal concepts. Also, the social nature of religious groupings creates connections between words and meanings that differ from one group to the next.

For the purposes of this chapter, I want to define what I mean by "spirit" or "spiritual." While Chapter Six pointed us toward issues of the soul—the mind, the will and the emotions—this chapter references another aspect of the human being—the spirit—or *the essence of identity*. It is the part of our being that is connected to and receives empowerment from the Divine nature.

In my first book, *Think Differently Live Differently,* I illustrated the idea of spirit by describing a dead body on a table slowly coming to life as spirit entered the body. Jesus described it this way: "You hear the sound of it, but you do not see the wind, where it comes from or where it goes." He pointed to the fact that man's spirit is invisible and more readily known for what it *does* than what it *is*.

Let's make it personal though and applicable to us as teachers and speakers. Let's examine how the things we receive, contain, and broadcast to our listeners *relates to* the Spirit of God.

HOW DO YOU RELATE?

Try this experiment with me.

Raise your hand and think for a moment. Some part of your being runs your life. When you have a decision to make, a problem to solve or even when you make plans for next week, some part of you does this for you. Take your upraised hand and place it on the part of you that runs your life. If it's taking you a moment to figure out where to put your hand, move it to your head. Your prolonged thinking gave you away.

Now that you have located this executive branch of your being, turn your full attention toward this part. Turn your thoughts and focus to whatever part of your being runs your life.

Now be honest. With your attention focused on the place from which your life runs, what do you *experience*? What do you *feel*? Make note if the feeling is positive or negative. Do you feel heaviness? Pressure? Peace? What do you feel?

Now raise your hand again. When the first part of your being isn't coming through for you and you have a decision to make or a problem to solve, what part of you engages next? What is your back-up plan when the first part fails?

Move your hand to this second part of your being. Now repeat the secondary exercise above. Turn all of your focus toward this part of you. After dwelling on this second part of your being, consider your experience or feeling now.

Again, is it positive or negative?

I have done this experiment in group settings, and I have seen that the most common locations people run their lives from are their mind (hand on their head) or their heart (hand on chest). I get a few variations, but overwhelmingly people acknowledge that they experience feelings of heaviness or anxiety when they focus on those areas. In fact, 80% or more report negative feelings.

So let's take a third step. Raise your hand one more time. Ask God where you are most aware of His Spirit inside you. Take your time. As you become aware move your hand to that place. And as before, turn your full attention to that part of your being. Now what do you experience?

Many people find their hands move to just above their navel, the place that moves your breath in and out. When people turn their attention to this place in their being, often a group can feel the atmosphere in the room shift. People report feeling peace and empowerment. They have located this mysterious thing called "spirit."

So let me ask you: What do you feel? What shift happens when you make this connection?

Now take one final step. Ask this place where you sense God in you to *speak* to the first two places you had focused on. Be still and let God's Spirit address your soul. What do you hear or sense? This exercise gives you a sense of what it means to "live by the spirit."

What do I mean by "spirit?" I mean that part of your being that either connects or is designed to connect to the storehouse of God's breath in the human soul. When we live and broadcast from this place we "live by the Spirit." It is the part of you that God inhabits as He moves you from simply being "not dead" to being fully alive. It is the source of human identity.

The spirit, then, is that place inside of us that is most connected to God and is designed to be the place of His residence. It is our source of "aliveness" beyond heartbeat, brain activity, and nervous system function. The Spirit is God in us, but also in union with us. It is us, but it is the part of us that is connected to "the Spirit outside of us."

> **"INTELLECT ALONE WILL ALWAYS MISCONSTRUE SPIRITUAL TRUTH."**

Spirit is more than our source of aliveness; it is truly our source of "us-ness." Spirit is our seat and source of identity. It is the energy inside us that moves us from biology to personhood. The writer of Genesis calls it the Breath of Life. The Apostle Paul calls it the Spirit. It is the life of God inside us, wrapped in and either restrained by, or released through, the human soul.

As I say in my second book, *Think Differently Lead Differently,* we are designed to live "from God" not "for God," and if this is the case, God must both reside in and move through us. We are designed with this capacity and designed to move and be moved from this place. If we are designed to be moved from this place, imagine the power when we learn to communicate from and to this place called "spirit."

Neil T. Anderson has said, "Head speaks to head and heart speaks to heart." I would add to that, "Spirit speaks to spirit."

To paraphrase the verse quoted at the beginning of this chapter, spiritual things can only be taken in and comprehended by the spirit within. Intellect alone will always misconstrue spiritual truth.

It is one thing to learn to listen with and through your spirit so that you might receive spiritual truth. It is another thing altogether to learn to speak from the Spirit. As a speaker or teacher who intends to help people in their personal transformation, learning to speak from your spirit is crucial. Certain groups would call this process "the anointing."

ANOINTED ON PURPOSE

Anointed is a term used in some faith communities and, like the word "spiritual" is another term that can be intended or received in a variety of ways. For our purposes, I define "anointed" as *operating under spiritual influence.*

I have heard this term used to describe people, moments, songs, and messages. All of these can be legitimate uses, and I believe most people mean that they have some experience of God beyond just the ideas or words being spoken.

I have also heard this term used as if it is a mystical visitation, outside the control of humans, that some people have and others do not. In this belief system, we must wait on the "fickle" will of God and then flock to those who have mysteriously received this thing called "anointing."

But… What if we could be anointed *on purpose?* What if we could learn to connect with and operate under the influence of God's Spirit *intentionally* while helping others do the same?

Years ago, I taught a weekly Sunday School class at a Baptist church. I developed a rhythm. Starting on Monday, I would seek direction from the Lord, by Wednesday the lesson would begin to take shape, and on Sunday, I would present what the Lord had given me. My communication with Him involved two-way prayer, scripture reading and meditation. This rhythm worked well for an extended time. Then one day, I sensed the Lord asking me what I would do if He didn't give me anything to teach.

I was taken aback by the question. Why wouldn't He give me something? I have a class to teach, right? I considered His question to be rhetorical and gave Him the "right" answer. "Of course, Lord, if You didn't give me anything, I just wouldn't teach."

Having passed the test, I went on with my routine and the next few weeks seemed to support that His question had simply been a rabbinical teaching strategy. He asked, I pondered. Lesson learned, right!?

Then a few weeks down the road, our conversation became one-sided. I still approached Him. I opened the Scriptures. He, however, seemed distracted (at least that's how I saw it!). It was as if He wasn't worried about whether or not I had material to teach.

This didn't cause me a great deal of stress until Wednesday arrived and He still hadn't spoken to me. I began to wonder why He might be waiting to give me my lesson for the week. By Friday, I remembered His question. That's when I began to worry.

I had a class to teach, and people expected me to have something important to say. It was my responsibility. I pushed Him harder. Perhaps He hadn't heard me. I also started thinking about what I could teach if He didn't give me anything.

I considered clever things and deep things and other things that I had either done before or knew something about. I considered what I could do if He didn't come through for me, and I seriously contemplated going on without Him if He gave me nothing. My students didn't need to know, and I felt sure I could fake my way through it.

Therein lies the problem for all of us. We can fake our way through. We can make things happen with or without God. In the right (or wrong) setting, where people have expectations, the pressure may exist to go ahead and present things or do something without Him. If we can, we eventually will, and if we will, we eventually do.

Sunday morning came, and the teaching hour approached. I still had nothing except two lessons I knew I could do without God. A tug of war waged inside me.

Should I teach without Him?

The moment came, and I stood up and paused. I didn't decide exactly what to do until that very moment. I looked at the 40 people who expected me to teach and told them, "I spent the week asking God what to teach, and He didn't give me anything."

They all watched me, still waiting for me to teach something. It was a little uncomfortable.

I continued, "So my current plan is to ask you guys if any of *you* heard something from God this week."

It only took a few awkward seconds…then two different people spoke up. The discussion that followed was some of the richest, most thought-provoking, growth-stimulating conversation we'd ever had in that class. More importantly, that day convinced me that it was *safe* to let God be in charge. I did not need to go on without Him to fulfill the expectations of a group.

I also believe that day changed my experience with God working through my teaching. I didn't get smarter, but I did realize that I was more than just my mind. With that realization, it seemed that more of His breath was present in our midst.

The first key to being anointed on purpose is to be certain that you will not go on without His empowering Spirit. I have heard a saying among speakers: "If you can't be anointed, at least be excited."

I couldn't disagree more.

Said another way, "If you can't be anointed, substitute what people need from God for something from your own nature or personality."

Our willingness to depend on our own strengths and style may be the greatest obstacle to receiving His strength. It is often our willingness, or even our expectation, to use *our* energy, *our* intelligence or *our* other human strengths that prevent us from operating in spiritual strength. If you refuse to go on without God, then He is more likely to inhabit what you are doing.

The next key to being anointed on purpose is to teach from hearing.

Earlier, we did an exercise that I often use to help people make a distinction between soul and spirit. Once this distinction is made, the next step is to help people learn to operate from that part of them where God dwells.

> **"THE FIRST KEY TO BEING ANOINTED ON PURPOSE IS TO BE CERTAIN THAT YOU WILL NOT GO ON WITHOUT HIS EMPOWERING SPIRIT."**

Take the time to connect with the spirit inside you. Listen first, then speak. If the message you deliver is one that God gave you, then let Him give it to you again as you deliver it. If you can learn to teach from hearing, you also increase the connection of your spirit to your words.

This principle reminds me of baseball. The number one rule in batting practice is to let the ball come to you. It is as much a mental posture as it is a physical act. It keeps muscles loose and subtly shifts the point of focus. It also gives a miniscule extra distance for adjustment as the ball comes closer.

Similarly, when teaching or speaking, let the words come to you. Teach from hearing. This act is as much psychological as it is spiritual, and it gives that extra bit of distance between your thoughts and your tongue for God to slip in.

Another key to being anointed on purpose is to learn to look through God's eyes as you speak. Remember that the people you address are men and women that He loves and died for.

When trying to be anointed on purpose, it is important to know that I am not suggesting that we can control the Spirit of God any more than I would suggest a surfer can control a wave. Instead, I suggest that God is eager to move through people, and our mental and spiritual posture can either prepare us for the move of God or prevent it.

Improvisation, a thought process we will discuss in Chapter Ten, is the act of taking what your left brain has learned and yielding it to a flow of creativity from the right brain. It is this yielding of thought process that lies at the heart of "teaching from hearing," allowing God to add to and stir what you know.

These internal adjustments can all lead to operating intentionally under the influence of God's Spirit while communicating. When you speak from the spirit, you broadcast spiritual truth and connect to the spiritual nature of your listeners.

But what of the act of *learning* spiritual truth? What is happening on the receiving end? And where do you get spiritual truth in the first place? Let's turn our eyes toward the process of revelation.

REVELATION

The kennel in our master bedroom was a new addition as was the eight-week-old puppy sleeping in it. It had been years since I had babies in my house, but once again, I was waking up in the middle of the night to a crying baby (animal). Our room had been newly furnished and night after night, I was still learning my way around the needs of this little creature as well as the new layout of our room where this little one slept.

I stumbled through the obstacle course without light to guide my way, bracing myself for any objects on the floor—or worse, the unexpected encounter of my toes or shins with the new kennel. Then it dawned on me. My smart phone could illuminate the room enough that I could successfully navigate the unfamiliar terrain.

As I turned on the screen, the room around me was revealed dimly at first but with enough contrast that I could avoid any painful encounters. All it took was a little light to reveal what was right in front of me.

Revelation is the process by which our spirit and mind develop or receive an awareness of the truths that are right in front of us but hidden by the absence of spiritual light. If spiritual things can only be spiritually learned, then we must not only speak from our spirit, but we must also learn to *learn* with our spirit.

Revelation is the process by which spiritual truth from God comes to the mind of a man or woman. Revelation can either help us receive new thoughts or change the way we see and experience thoughts we already have.

Like the thought processes described in Chapter Two, revelation is a way that the mind processes. The biggest difference is that revelation is not an internal thought process; it is a relational thought process. It comes *to* your mind, not *from* your mind.

Revelation is something you can prepare yourself for, but you cannot manufacture or harness it. The relationship between a teacher and God's revelatory voice is like the relationship between a surfer and the ocean.

The surfer must learn how to read the ocean and select a wave. Once the wave is selected, he must learn to position himself to ride on top and slightly above the power of the wave. The surfer doesn't generate any power; he simply learns how to position himself to ride it.

As we learn to tune into God's presence and voice, we must learn how to recognize His patterns and position ourselves to ride His wave too. Whether in our private time as God speaks and teaches us, or in public as we share what we've learned, we must rely as much on His breath to bring life to our words as we did for His breath to bring words to our minds.

When we ask God to open up His Scriptures to us, we can see and hear new things in new ways. Receiving this kind of personal enlightenment or revelation prepares us to teach not simply from the place of our intellect, but also to shine light around us because of the light shone in us.

This process turns teaching from a study-organize-present model to a receive-contain-broadcast model. This kind of revelation implicitly teaches others the value of their own connection to God's Spirit. As we learn to trust this process, we also learn that it is an inhale and exhale process. We learn to receive revelation, and in that same way, we learn to broadcast.

This was the case for James, one of our *Think Differently Live Differently* workshop attendees. After one of our exercises, he jumped out of the chair and ran around the room as if he had won the lottery. He pumped his fist in the air and kept repeating, "Yes, I knew it! I knew it!" He ran and jumped some more and then shouted again, "Yes, yes!!! I knew it!"

We had just finished learning to receive and broadcast the things God says or shows us. James had been on the receiving end, and his exercise partner had just leaned over and whispered a single word into his ear. It was this word that propelled him from his chair.

The assignment instructed James to ask God for something he needed. He had spent two minutes in silence, asking and focusing on the thing he wanted from God.

His partner for this exercise was assigned to ask God what James needed. As assigned, he asked what one word God wanted to say to James after two minutes of silent eye contact and listening.

When James finally caught his breath from all the excitement, he told us what had happened. "I only want one thing," he said. "I spent the entire two minutes saying, 'Please God, I just need more confidence.' For two minutes I asked that as many times as I possibly could. When my partner leaned over, he said one word, 'Confidence.'"

It was this moment of revelation that launched James into orbiting the room a time or two. I have watched this exercise dozens of times, and the amazing ways that God speaks always surprises me. James' story wasn't even the most amazing; it was just the most exuberant.

Revelation is the source of all faith (*Faith comes by hearing…*). It is the source of all life (*He breathed the breath of life into his nostrils…*). It is the source of all planets (*And God said let there be…*), and it is the source of all truth.

Revelation is the weapon that destroys strongholds. If transformation is our goal and the restoration of human identity is the target, then revelation is the way.

A LITTLE HELP?

It all comes down to this: When dealing with the spiritual side of communication, we are not only employing strategies or thought processes, we are also learning to partner with God in our communication. We don't control revelation, nor are we at the mercy of hopelessly waiting on random downloads. We can reach out to Him for help. Since we don't control revelation, just be prepared for the help to look different than you might have expected.

Though our office is a counseling center that holds classes as well as personal and professional training, we have a team of prayer intercessors. Their job is to stay aware of all our events and circumstances, both personal and professional, and pray for God's work in all we do. Since the spiritual world doesn't shut down at 5 p.m., their vigilance is paramount. I always say we need to win the air war before we proceed with the ground war. We never doubt that God is willing and eager to be at work among us and that our posture of expecting and asking connects His willingness to our need.

The posture of need and expectancy are an important part of preparing the way for God to empower your communication. It is also an important part of preparing the way for God to empower your listeners.

Almost every time I speak in public, the prayer I begin with is Ephesians 1:17-19. This is the prayer Paul prayed for the Ephesian church. He asked, as do I, that God would open the eyes of the hearts and grant the Spirit of wisdom and revelation to those who hear.

I pray this regularly for myself and my listeners. I pray this not as a formula that God must respond to; rather, I pray this from a place of realizing that we are asking for God to do more than my limited teaching can accomplish. The nature of spiritual communication relies on God's empowerment. I have prayed that over this book.

Everything you have read in these pages has dozens of applications and implications. In the next chapter, you will find more as we discover how to really connect with an audience. Then in Chapter Ten, we will peek together into the

> **"THE NATURE OF SPIRITUAL COMMUNICATION RELIES ON GOD'S EMPOWERMENT."**

tool chest. Of course, no tool can substitute for integration and vulnerability. No tool can counterfeit genuine compassion. There is no strategy to manufacture love for the people you reach. Not a single technique exists to make you choose to surrender to the Breath of God as the source of your hearing and your broadcasting.

You are a teacher.

Whether you teach your friends and family by being you or if you stand on a platform and speak to crowds, you are a teacher. You do not teach topics, you teach people.

I pray these pages have breathed life into you and prepared you to breathe life into others. And I pray that God would open the eyes of your heart and grant you the Spirit of wisdom and revelation. Let's now look into the power of Divine connection.

STUDY GUIDE

KEY CONCEPTS

- Man is both material and spiritual.

- Spirit is the part of you that is designed to be connected to God.

- Being anointed means operating under a spiritual influence.

- Hearing from God and seeing through His eyes helps you be anointed on purpose

- Revelation is the way spiritual truth comes from God to man.

SKILL BUILDERS

1. Repeat the exercise where you find God's Spirit in you several times this week. Practice shifting your attention from soul to Spirit.

2. Ask God questions this week and wait for answers. Don't ask questions that you know the answer to.

3. When you get comfortable locating the Spirit inside you, let that part show you the people in your life.

CHAPTER 9

CONNECTING WITH YOUR AUDIENCE

Your assumptions are your windows on the world. Scrub them off every once in a while, or the light won't come in.
—Isaac Asimov

I made mistakes in drama. I thought drama was when actors cried. But drama is when the audience cries.
—Frank Capra

I sat in a circle with the worship team, each of them trying to be still and ask God what He wanted to say to us. I had given them the same instructions I had on many other occasions when I taught people or groups about learning to hear and discern God's voice.

I had told them to still their minds and turn their attention toward God's Presence in the room. As they settled into stillness, I instructed them to pay attention to anything that entered their minds. I told them that as they sensed, saw or heard things, together we would discern if it was God's voice and what it might mean. I gave a quick teaching on the ways God spoke to men in the Bible and then urged them to wait in silence.

After a few moments of silence, the leader of the team looked up at me like he had something to say. He looked a little nervous and unsure, but he spoke anyway. "You told us that even if it doesn't make sense to say out loud what we believe we have heard, right?"

"Right," I said. "Sometimes God may bring the whole group together by giving one a word but another an interpretation. When He does this, He not only conveys His message, but He also fosters unity."

"OK," he said, looking right at me. "I am pretty sure I heard this, but it makes no sense to me. Not only that, but it feels like it is specifically for you."

Now it was my turn to feel anxious. You never know what's coming next! When I heard His words, they made immediate sense, and I knew it was God. To this day, I will never forget the message or the moment. The words were simple. The specificity and the meaning were profound.

My friend looked right at me and said, "I feel like God is saying to you, 'Always remember the second service revelation.' Does that make any sense?"

In that moment I felt both seen and known by the God who spoke to my friend. Not only did it make sense, it impacted me profoundly. I hadn't told anyone. It had occurred in a private moment, and I had kept the revelation to myself. But it had happened in that very room, less than 20 feet from where we sat in our circle.

Two weeks earlier, I had spoken at that church. It had been the first time I had spoken to such a large group. The room was packed, but this time 1,200 people were waiting for me to speak. When I stood on that stage, all my clever thoughts and confident words drained out in the anxiety of facing the sea of people.

I made my way through my talk, but I felt that at best, I had stumbled—at worst, I had failed. Frozen in my nervousness, I had felt every stutter and misstep as if each one had been fatal. And all that had happened in the first service. There was still one yet to go.

As the music began ushering us into the second service, I began mentally preparing to do the best I could so as not to fail again. Of course, I did all the wrong things. The worst way to overcome self-consciousness is to focus on yourself. But for 20 minutes of the 25-minute worship set, all I could do was focus on me, myself, and I.

Then my thoughts were interrupted. A calming voice seemed to break through my anxiety, and as the words washed over my mind, everything inside me settled.

God spoke.

"Bob," He said, "when you stand up to speak this time, take a moment. Look out at all those people and see each of them as people that I love and have died for."

Not only did I settle down on the inside before I got up to speak, but when I stood up and faced the sea of humanity, I took a breath and looked directly into the faces of the crowd. Some were friends. Some were new to me. All of them were loved, and I was there to be a part of something bigger than my talk. I was there to step into something that Jesus had accomplished two thousand years ago. In that moment of silence, God's love for them became mine as well.

Without a trace of anxiety, I began to tell those men and women about the healing love of God. I became a conduit for the very thing that I spoke about. It was a revelation that not only set me free in the moment, but it has affected the way I see and think from that point onward.

Then weeks later, in an intimate setting, God confirmed and affirmed this in the cleverest way. His powerful lesson: "Never forget the second service revelation." Not only have I never forgotten it, but I also believe no one who wants to introduce real change to humanity should ever forget it.

WHAT ARE WE TEACHING?

When we speak publicly—whether we do so on a regular basis or have a single opportunity—it is crucial to remember we are not teaching topics. We are teaching *people*. Regardless of what we have to say or how important it is, our target is never great delivery. Our target is people.

> "REGARDLESS OF WHAT WE HAVE TO SAY OR HOW IMPORTANT IT IS, OUR TARGET IS NEVER GREAT DELIVERY. OUR TARGET IS PEOPLE."

We must first enter into the lives of people with our own lives. If the method and the message are to be congruent, then it is important to recognize that any time we intend to convey a message of transformation, the method must always include incarnation.

Ultimately, the right-brained approach is not merely about creativity and abstract methodology. It is about connection. It is about what takes place between humans during the process of communication. Regardless of how true or how important our messages are, if we disconnect from others, the message falls flat like the data sent on a fading WiFi signal.

The primary message and foundation of all communication begins with what we convey through our posture toward and our connection with people. It is here that we convey to what degree we value the people in front of us.

People will know, either consciously or unconsciously, if we value them or if we are simply delivering content. In certain settings, content delivery is sufficient. However, if facilitating change is our goal—especially meaningful transformation—people must know we value them. If we remain disconnected from them while we talk about life-changing principles, we inadvertently convey that change is about improved performance rather than about deeper connection.

We love to say that our belief in God is about relationship not religion. However, if we remain disconnected from those we say this to, then our method of disconnection becomes a more powerful message than the words we speak. This echoes back to the covert and overt communication we talked about back in Chapter Two. If they're not in sync, we've lost our connection and our ability to instigate change in people's lives.

One of the most important aspects of life-changing communication is the relational aspect. This chapter will discuss two primary issues: First, our relationship to our words and message, and second, our relationships to the people with whom we communicate.

YOUR MESSAGE AND YOU

The book of Proverbs speaks often about motive, and how much God is concerned with motive. I believe the reason for this is simple. God is concerned about integrity—not simply integrity as defined by our relationship to truth and honesty, but rather integrity as defined by integration or congruence. God is deeply interested and even invested in our *integration*.

By integration, I mean that every part of our being is in unity with every other part, inside and out. When we are integrated, we are the same on the inside as we are on the outside. In many ways, this is a crucial part of living a life of freedom and wholeness. Therefore, it is always a part of any communication about change.

I have observed in my counseling practice that, among people who lie habitually, one of the most consistent motives for lying is people-pleasing. People face the dilemma of whether to speak about what they *wish* were true or about what *is* true.

As contrary as that seems, a people pleaser will almost always say what brings the most positive response *in the moment*. They do so to create the most positive response by either making someone happy or keeping them from being hurt or upset regardless of what is actually true.

If their words are untrue, soon time and circumstance will reveal the deceptiveness of their statement. It was the war on the inside of their soul that led them to lie. While some part of them knew better, another part needed the positive response of the moment. They were not integrated, and as a result, their inner man and their outer man had two different presentations.

What happens then if we teach or communicate something that we, ourselves, don't live? Or something that we are disconnected from? What happens when we reteach old material simply because we must have something to say? What happens when any message we speak in any setting comes from a place inside of us that is not meaningfully connected to our words?

Once during a teacher training, I asked each teacher to speak and then receive input from the class. One of the participants got up and shared a deeply personal, frightening, and painful experience. She seemed honest. All her information was accurate. She seemed emotional in that she didn't feel disconnected from the room.

But somehow, it seemed that her feelings were not as strong as the reality of the story she shared. I asked her how recent the story was, and it was quite recent. I asked her if she had feelings about it that were stronger than what she was sharing in the room.

She paused. In her pause, she looked inward, and we could feel her change. As she changed, the room changed. I suggested she stay connected and tell us again. She said she thought she needed to control her feelings in order to be effective. I simply asked her to connect to what was real.

As she repeated the exact same story a second time, it was as if she were telling a brand-new story. This time it was *her* and her story, not just a story. She reached us all with the depth of her experience.

This woman with a powerful story had assumed that, if she controlled her emotions, she could be clearer about her message. But in truth, when she disconnected from her emotions, she disconnected from her story. Far more than her ideas, *she* was the power of her story.

If not careful, one might mistakenly assume that the message of this section is to share emotions in order to influence people. But the message is not about what you portray on the outside. The message is about the *integration* between the inside and the outside. If we share emotions outwardly that are incongruent with the inside, we can be manipulating our listeners, and there is no integrity in manipulation.

The first and most important relational issue in transformational communication is that we must remain connected to ourselves when we speak.

The second is that we must connect to others.

TEACHING THROUGH CONNECTION—NOT TOPICS

His timing made it difficult. He could only come late in the day. My timing didn't help either. I had recently experienced some personal tragedy, and my emotional stamina was low. He needed help with his anger, and he trusted me to help him. He had suffered a lifetime of betrayal, and his anger now pushed people away, making him feel all the more betrayed.

I knew he needed help, but between my low stamina and the hardness of his anger, I found myself giving him the easiest thing to give: Answers. I drew diagrams and talked about strategies. I gave coping and emotional management plans. I gave him lots of information. I knew he needed more.

After a few sessions, I knew something had to change. Stamina or no, I knew he needed a human connection. Information and strategy wasn't even touching the place he needed help. He was in pain, and I was giving him ideas.

> **"HE DID NOT NEED ANSWERS. HE NEEDED ANOTHER HUMAN TO MEET HIM IN THE PLACE OF HIS DESPAIR."**

Finally, I took a deep breath and decided to sit with him and connect with him in his pain. He began his usual routine of reciting his frustrations. It was tempting to once again hide behind ideas. I stayed with him and began to express empathy. "That must have been terribly painful," I voiced.

He slowed for a moment and went on.

"I am so sorry," I empathized. "You must have been so hurt."

He slowed again. He softened a bit. "Yeah," he said, "I was."

He went on and so did I. I was committed to stay with him.

"And then she left me too…" he uttered.

I leaned in again and made eye contact. Sad for his rejection, I said, "I am so sorry, it must feel like nobody loved you…"

He stopped. He looked at me, eyes moist. "You know what's the worst part?"

"What?"

"*I* don't love me. The worst part is that *I* don't love me, and I am *stuck* with me."

And now our work could begin.

He did not need answers. He needed another human to meet him in the place of his despair. No cognitive answer could have gotten him to the place where connection naturally took us.

I can't stress this enough: Always, always connect.

SETTING UP YOUR PLATFORM FOR CONNECTION

We sat for five minutes in silence. He stared at me. His face and his posture dared me to get him to speak. Only an hour before, I had sat in the same chair but in a completely different connection. The client in that hour had had high expectations that I was exactly the right person to help him. Two different people, and to them, I occupied two different platforms.

The people we speak with have assigned us a place in their lives, and every word they hear from us comes from the platform we occupy. No matter how brilliant or awkward our words are, the primary filter people hear through depends on who we are in *their* world, not who they are in ours.

Parents occupy a different platform with their eight-year-old than they do with the same child six years later. And hopefully, they occupy an entirely different platform again after the passage of adolescence.

Let's consider some questions that every communicator must ask himself or herself:

- Who are we to our listeners?

- Is there resistance (or barriers) to us and our message, or is acceptance already established?

- Does our platform in our listeners' lives predispose them to a particular way of hearing us?

Before we deliver our messages, we must establish some place of validity and connection in the minds and consideration of our listeners. And as we establish our places, we should watch for signs to indicate the platform we have gained.

If we speak to a group who already has knowledge and expectation of what we can offer them, we may be able to move much more quickly into the core message.

If the audience doesn't know us and doesn't know what to expect, we should take the time to build our platforms by starting with where we believe they are and gently moving to where we want them to be.

When I speak to audiences, I want them to expect to stop and think. I want them to anticipate shifts, and I want them to expect that they will hear something they haven't heard before. I want them to expect those things as soon as possible.

If I am brand new to them, I have a few jokes that I tell with unexpected punch lines that shift their perspective. I change details of the joke to fit the culture I am in. If I can, I will use names of people that I have met in the room before I speak. These strategies are intended to establish the platform I am after. I want them to believe that I can shift their thinking, so I try to do it early even if the shift comes through a simple punch line.

If I don't use a joke and it is my first time to address a particular group, I often start with a specific teaching that is designed to shift thought process, and I try to shift things fairly quickly. Using a series of questions and quick illustrations, I want to grab their minds immediately.

The shift I like to use most begins with this question: "What if the problem that Jesus came to solve makes it very likely that we will misunderstand the problem Jesus came to solve?"

The question is designed to be a little confusing and to stop their thought process. I quickly follow by saying, "Let me illustrate what I mean this way: If I lose my glasses, I don't only have one problem. I have two. The first problem I have is easy to see." I hold up my glasses. "The problem is that I have lost my glasses. The second problem is the one most people don't think of right away."

All of this is designed to both slow and turn their thought process. After a pause, I say, "The second problem is that *the way* I find lost things (pause) is what I have lost."

After another long pause, while I watch to see responses, I say, "What if what Adam and Eve lost in the garden was more than a connection to God, what if they lost their way of knowing?"

Through this introduction, I do my best to set up a platform where the audience begins to expect to think differently. I know that this is the platform I want. This technique and others are the focus of the next chapter.

The bottom line is this: Know what platform you want and develop strategies to get your listeners to that place before you start to deliver anything else.

BEGIN BY LISTENING

If everything is communication (and it is), then communication is not only what we say, but also our propensity to hear.

If we intend to send a message that finds a deep target within our listeners, then we must first send a message that we are willing to receive ourselves. Our willingness to hear and receive from others sends two very important messages.

First, it is a powerful statement of value. In a world of communication overkill, everyone wants to find a new way to transmit. Every medium and every new strategy becomes fair game for people or organizations to send their message(s). With such an emphasis on transmission, consider the counterintuitive message sent by taking the time to listen instead.

> **"ATTENDING TO THE WORDS, HEART, AND WORLDVIEW OF ANOTHER IS A DEEP STATEMENT OF VALUE AND LOVE."**

No greater statement of value or love exists than taking the time to silently, empathically, and genuinely listen— not the kind of listening that is actually just waiting our turn without talking. Attending to the words, heart, and worldview of another is a deep statement of value and love.

Second, taking the time to truly listen models genuine listening. Listening is a lost art. When someone experiences the impact of being heard and sees the way the communicator practiced it, it can change the way that they stop, listen, and receive.

While much of this book is about ways to use words to change others, we can allow *our* value of *their* words to be a mechanism of change too. Our willingness to listen allows the words of others to become more powerful because they receive a place of true value. Our silence and listening ears are loud statements of connection.

If we are set to address a large group, we can make meaningful connections with the people in the room by showing up early and spending time with them. Even if we can't connect with everyone, the group will see that we value people and are there to teach people not topics.

IT'S NOT ABOUT THE SPEAKER

One dynamic of communication that is important but sometimes abstract is whether or not the communication is about the speaker or about the listeners. I have found that it is possible to talk about myself while still making my message about others. In the same way, it would be easy to talk about others while still making the message about myself.

Yes, personal stories are important. They are as much a part of the conversation as we are, and we should tell them. However, as much as those stories can be effective techniques, they can also become barriers to helping people change. It all depends on how we use them.

The story that says, "I am like you" or "I am with you" is an automatic rapport-building strategy. The story that says, "I did it right you should too" or worse, "Look how good I am," shuts down our listeners. The difference between the two is more about our hearts than our words, but both heart and words matter.

People already naturally struggle with shame or fear of inadequacy. When a story makes us look good, it leans toward the implication that others are not as good as us. If this is the message our listeners receive, we do harm instead of good.

If our stories demonstrate vulnerability or humility, however, we can draw people out of hiding and into connection. Sharing stories where we learned or grew, or stories where we struggled, builds bridges between us and our audience.

We can ask ourselves this question: *Is my motivation for telling this story to connect with people or to be admired?* If we're not sure, we can play out our talk in our minds as if we tell the story without identifying our role in it. If we find ourselves wanting to slip in that the story is about us, then we have our answer.

To remedy this, we can tell our stories or illustrations as if they are about someone else. Then we can read our hearts during and after. This is such an important aspect of all relationships. The skill of making communication about others is one that I teach married couples in therapy.

When we talk about someone else but our motive is still validation, we have still made the communication about us.

"Honey I know how much you love flowers and how much you love having the dishes finished. I also know how much you love not having to worry about the plans for the evening."

While that message sounds like it is focused on the needs of the spouse, it can subtly be more about the needs of the speaker if the implication is "I did this, validate me." Generous words can have a selfish effect.

The subject of the sentence is not necessarily the subject of the communication. This is deeply important because communication that is always only self-focused will eventually diminish the relationship and place a barrier between the speaker and the listener.

> **"EVERYTHING IS COMMUNICATION."**

From a platform, a speaker can tell his or her own story and maintain a real focus on the audience. When the motive is to help those in the audience, it comes out in a hundred ways because *everything is communication.*

RAPPORT

Rapport is a synchronization of souls and is vital to ensure that your message will be received. It functions like tuning two instruments together before they are used to play a duet. Without it, the most skilled musicians cannot play together, and without rapport, the most important context for communication has yet to be established.

Rapport is far more than simply establishing value or immediate connection with others. Rapport is the deep connection that allows you to synchronize your internal representations with those of the audience.

In NLP, rapport is described as the feeling of being in sync with someone, to truly be understood by them, and to feel that you understand them. At first glance, NLP practitioners will offer a set of skills to gain rapport. Matching and mirroring as well as leading and pacing are skills that are taught to help build rapid and powerful rapport.

These skills essentially develop the ability to match subtle attributes, behaviors, and postures of others, or even to a roomful of people. The skills are built on a foundation of observation and sensory acuity that sharpens the ability to notice the subtler cues of another person's state and presence.

When skilled communicators use these tools, people say things like, "I feel like we really click," or "I really feel like you get me." It is as simple as creating an impression that the communicators are like the people they're addressing. When they match and mirror listeners, everyone benefits from the universal experience that we all are the most comfortable around and the most connected to people who are most like us.

THE PITFALLS OF MANIPULATION

A common response I hear when bringing up communication models like NLP is the fear of the negative use of these techniques for manipulation. I share that fear with any technique that can influence people's thinking and beliefs. I have concerns that every technique in this book could potentially be used for manipulative purposes.

Similarly, I have concerns that the practice of spiritual gifts can be used for manipulation. Preaching and knowledge of the Scripture can all be used to manipulate others. When it comes to manipulating, nothing is more powerful than equating our words to God's words and God's will.

As a therapist I have learned a number of tools that can powerfully influence people. Here is my stance on this issue.

Manipulation is, *in itself,* not negative or positive. Chiropractors are asked to manipulate people when their skeletal and nervous systems are impinged in some way. According to *Webster's Dictionary*, manipulation, in its purest meaning, is to treat or operate something as if with the hands, or to operate in a skillful manner.

Manipulation becomes a problem when the goal is selfish gain instead of the good of a client or listener. Just as people are impinged in their physical conditions, people can be stuck in their cognitive or emotional traps. A skilled therapist can apply pressure to a cognitive trap and release a mind from its own impingement.

It is for this reason that therapists are subject to ethical codes. Rules are set in place to protect people from using the advantageous position and skill set of a therapist for their own benefit. For this reason, a therapist cannot benefit financially from his clients other than through the established fee structure. Financial gifts are not allowed nor are dual relationships that might benefit the therapist and cost the client.

Sadly, while we see the same power dynamics in the church/ministry world, the ethical standard can be non-existent or even reversed. People on platforms and in positions of influence are encouraged to ask for financial gifts. If these gifts benefit those who need help it is very different than when a speaker asks for money for selfish gain or expects to receive special favors. The ethic exists in counseling to keep motivations pure and lines of communication wide open. Asking for or expecting special favors can actually change the way people receive your message.

Manipulation is a heart issue and is a danger in every exchange. It is especially a danger when there is a power differential because of position or influence. No ethical code is sufficient to guard against it. The protection against manipulation is the responsibility of those with power to guard their own hearts against selfishness.

The value of learning powerful transformational communication skills is that it can help people. Like many tools, if they can help, they can also hurt. It is people and their motives that make the difference. We must always ask, "What's my motive?"

We began this chapter by saying that we are not teaching topics. We are teaching people. Our connection to our listeners or readers is the key context to make sure our message hits its target. We are now ready to bring together everything we have learned by exploring teaching techniques that help others achieve the change they so desperately desire and need.

STUDY GUIDE

KEY CONCEPTS

- We are teaching people before we are teaching topics.

- Tend to your relationship with yourself as well as others.

- It is important to know the platform you have in the eyes of your audience.

- Listening is always an important part of speaking.

- Rapport means being in sync with your audience.

- We must always ask, "What is my motive?"

SKILL BUILDERS

1. In your next conversation, pay attention to how often you want to speak. When you have the urge to speak, try not to and see how you feel. What can you surmise from this?

2. Try looking through the eyes of others this week. Literally consider what they might be seeing through their eyes.

3. Practice rapport-building in a one-on-one conversation. Match the other person's posture and tone. Match their pace. Notice how it affects them when you do this.

4. Learn one personal fact about each service person (cashier, waiter, mechanic …) you meet this week.

CHAPTER 10

13 STRATEGIES FOR SOUL-CHANGING COMMUNICATION

The task of the modern educator is not to cut down jungles, but to irrigate deserts.
—C.S. Lewis

I never teach my pupils. I only attempt to provide the conditions in which they can learn.
—Albert Einstein

Ideas lead to strategies, and conversely, strategies reveal ideas. This chapter will be different from the other chapters in that it will take all the ideas of the previous chapters and turn them into recipes. Here you'll find not only strategies to reach your audience, but also new ways to understand your audience. As you use them, you'll find that they illuminate and deepen the meta-thought processes we have been sifting through.

I encourage you to read through this entire chapter to familiarize yourself with these strategies, but then use this list as a resource you can "cherry pick" from whenever you're preparing to speak to an audience.

STRATEGY #1
PREPARING A ROADMAP

Let's begin with a well-known pre-communication strategy. In the same way that even the best seed needs to land in prepared soil in order to bear fruit, words have more impact when we have prepared the mind to receive.

We must remember that our hearers have not been on the same journey with us nor have they been inside our minds as we prepare. To maximize the impact of our words, we can bring them to a place of receptivity with relative ease.

It helps to be clear about where we believe our listeners are and where we want to take them as we begin to speak. If our listeners have all come in from a day's work or if they have all been sitting through a worship set, we must be in tune to their readiness to receive.

If context is a crucial part of how we want them to think, then we must take the time to set up context. We can't assume they will pick up on unspoken thoughts, so we must provide background. We can do this by giving them background for our own journeys or provide backgrounds for our ideas. Both help bring listeners to a receptive place.

If we know the kind of thought process we want to use or develop, then it is especially important to prepare them for this. Again, a story that requires the kind of thought process you are targeting can be very helpful. For example, the acrobat parable at the beginning of this book helps prepare readers for the lessons throughout—not only with its message, but also with the right-brain way the story is delivered.

Preparing the mind can be as simple as setting context before we verbalize our messages, but I believe it is more. Think of your message as seed and the minds of your listeners as soil. In every setting, the soil must be evaluated for its readiness—and the harvest will be maximized by effective soil preparation.

I like to tell people what they are likely to experience or how they might have to process what they are about to hear. I might say something like, "I am about to tell you something that will sound like something you have heard before. You will have to listen more carefully to discover what is new."

Such a statement prepares people to listen for more detail. The mind is prepared to work a bit more intently.

Or I might say, "I am about to tell you three stories *about* a story. Then I'm going to tell you some stories about a guy who teaches by telling stories."

A statement like this gives the mind both a roadmap and prepares it for the flavor of the upcoming message. The mind usually works from big picture to detail, or from whole to part. Providing a big picture on the front end helps the mind organize what follows.

As the classic speaker's advice goes, "Tell them what you are about to tell them. Tell them, and then tell them what you just told them." The mind wants a roadmap to follow. I might say it another way. Prepare the mind to receive what you want to tell them. Then tell them. Then water and nurture what you have told them.

Sometimes the best way to prepare a mind is to tell a few stories. Metaphors reach the structures in the mind whether the listener is conscious of it or not and a metaphorical story can be a great way to access the specific structures you want to access.

I worked with someone who had a hard time being present in the moment. I began our conversation having a simple conversation about my two dogs. I told him that my puppy is full of energy and loves life, that she is constantly scanning the horizon to figure out where else she might go.

I then told him that we also have a six-year-old dog and that in her maturity she still loves to run and play. She also enjoys being present in any given moment where someone might want to scratch her ears or give her a treat.

Doing so prepared his mind to receive the seed of remaining present to connect to some healthy changes he needed to make.

We must prepare others to receive our messages. We are the only ones who have been in our minds. At the beginning of our messages, we must help our hearers get to the same place that we are.

STRATEGY #2
LANGUAGE PATTERNS

If the mind is a computer and structures are its software, then language is, well, the programming language. All messages are part of the programming, but as mentioned in Chapter Three, language (or communication) can be a key to reprogramming a moment or a lifetime.

Language patterns set up the mind and can turn the mind in a given direction simply by using language *intentionally*. Sequenced wisely, words create a path that the mind will naturally follow. They convey any number of below-conscious directions the mind could go. Here are four examples of language patterns you can use in your communication:

LANGUAGE PATTERNS THAT CONVEY EXPECTANCY

Prior to any communication exchange, expectancy is already in place. Language patterns contain these expectancies, but they can also be used to set them in place or change them. Consider these examples:

- *"Not everybody here tonight will be completely changed."*

- While this may sound like a negative statement, listen again. The phrase, "not everybody," implies that some people will be changed. The expectancy, "Some of you here tonight will be completely changed," could meet resistance. Verbalized as an implication, it can slip in and raise some expectations, especially for those who may be resistant.

- *"After Buddy makes the shot, get back as fast as you can on defense."*

- This classic moment in the movie, *Hoosiers*, shows the coach using a language pattern to create an expectancy and to change the focal point of the team. In a high-pressure situation, he states a low-pressure expectancy that the young man *will* make the shot and then turns the focus of the team to another place to keep the pressure low.

- *"That's likely to pop in your mind unexpectedly without really trying at all."*

- When in a conversation with someone who is struggling to remember something, we can make this statement and take the pressure off. It suggests the expectation that his mind will find it when he stops trying.

My wife and I will play simple word games with this pattern, saying things like:

- *"I wonder when that is going to come back to you…"*

- *"I'll be curious to see how long it takes you to stop trying so hard…"*

- *"I am excited to see what that is like for you when you are on the other side of that (obstacle)."*

All of these patterns assume a simple expectancy. When speaking to others, we must listen to our words to see if we are telling them to do something or if we are telling them to expect something. As we listen to our language patterns, we can discover our own expectations. What do you hear in these two examples?

- *"I always lose things."*

- *"I am just going to mess it up again."*

Often when I hear people say things like "always" or "never," I push back to give them new expectancies.

"I never get that right," they utter.

"Wait a minute," I interrupt. "Say that again, but say, 'So far I have not gotten that right consistently.'"

By helping others change their language patterns, we help them change their thoughts. Watch to see what happens when you change your language patterns to a new expectancy.

LANGUAGE PATTERNS THAT CONVEY RESPONSIBILITY

Many people are stuck because they don't see they must be responsible for themselves; they want others to be responsible for them. Their language is a dead giveaway. Through language patterns, we can give them back the power they need.

- Statement: *"Let's go turn that off."*

- This statement, accompanied by a lack of action, conveys a passive or covert request for someone else to act.

- Response: "When you say that, do you mean me or you?"

- This response gives them the chance to be direct and take ownership of their ambiguity.

- Statement: *"There is no one to take me to the water when it is stirred."*

- This classic answer to Jesus by the crippled man at the pool of Bethesda is a response to the question, "Do *you want* to be made well?" Notice how he assumes other people are responsible for his frustration.

- Response: "What is it that you really want?"

- This question again makes the speaker take ownership and in his response urges him to assign responsibility directly instead of indirectly.

- Statement:*"Everybody is upset about that."*

- This usually is a way to express frustration without taking ownership.

- Response: "Are you upset about it?"

- This response again gives the speaker responsibility and, therefore, gives them back power.

- Statement: "This car is always such a mess."

- This observation is a general complaint but also has an implication of wanting someone else to solve the problem.

- Response: *"I wonder what you will do about it."*

- What a great response to give responsibility and ownership back to the person who is trying to avoid it!

People who don't accept responsibility cannot change. We must be sure that in both our language patterns and our work with others' language patterns that we help people accept their own responsibility.

LANGUAGE PATTERNS THAT CONVEY IDENTITY VERSUS BEHAVIOR

People often confuse their experiences with their identities. This is a common thought process that creeps its way into our daily language. You can help people who do this with a simple thought interruption.

- *"I am a worrier"* is an identity statement.

- *"I worry a lot"* is a behavior statement.

For people who have repeated or ongoing struggles, it is a constant trap to begin identifying themselves *by* their struggles. This kind of mindset is easy to spot, but we can help others experience meaningful change when we understand and communicate the distinction.

"I am a worrier," they say.

"Are you sure?" you might respond. "Is worrying *who you are* or just something *you have learned* to do?"

The implication here is not simply that worrying is a behavior, but rather that it is a *learned* behavior. Thankfully, any behavior that is learned can be unlearned.

By helping people change their language patterns, we can empower them to stop identifying their nature by their habits. Doing so will begin to erode structures that have worked against them.

LANGUAGE PATTERNS THAT CONVEY EXCEPTION VERSUS RULE

This is a derivative of the expectancy pattern. The difference is that it gets at the core of how people see themselves in both negative and positive experiences. People with negative expectancies see positive experiences as an exception. They minimize them in their mind and with language. They often over-emphasize negatives and under-emphasize, or downplay positives.

- *"Every time something good happens, something bad always follows. I have learned to not get too excited because I just wait for something bad to follow."*

- It is amazing how the mind has learned to punctuate that experience! So if they see the pattern as something good followed by something bad, I typically respond, "How do you know which one comes first? It sounds like it is just as true that when something bad happens you could just as easily be waiting for the good thing. They alternate, so how do you know that it's not just as true that after every bad thing happens something good is going to happen?"

There is freedom in helping people recognize that their pictures are expressed in their words, and their pictures may simply be framed in unhelpful ways.

STRATEGY #3
REFRAMING

In the movie, *The Greatest Showman,* P.T. Barnum reads a scathing report in the newspaper. The critic had done his best to paint the show as an abomination. Barnum's front gate man is deeply concerned about the effect this critique could have on their sales.

Barnum looks at him with a wink and assigns him a classic reframe. "Take out a full-page ad, reprint this review, and tell them everybody who brings it in gets half-price admission."

What could have diminished their value at the gate became a tool to increase sales—simply by reframing. Reframing is the assignment of a different meaning to an event or circumstance in order to change the impact or power that it has over those who have assigned meaning to it.

A commonly used reframe is the idea that problems are opportunities for solutions. Reframing is not a dishonest change of meaning. It is a change of perspective to empower others or shift the way they perceive a circumstance or idea.

I heard a well-known comedian once say that he developed his comedic thought process by looking at circumstances from different perspectives. Reframing accomplishes two things: One, it provides another way of seeing things, and two, it increases people's all-around mental flexibility.

Reframing takes on two different expressions. The first is to change the context and thereby change the meaning of the circumstance. The second is to directly change the meaning.

REFRAMING TO CHANGE THE CONTEXT

As I teach on strongholds or the areas where people struggle, I begin by shifting how people see their struggles. "Everything you struggle with is something that was invented by God for your well-being and is simply being used in the wrong way. Your struggles are not something wrong with you, rather they are something right with you that has been misapplied or misused."

The context of their problem is now finding what is right with their struggle instead of identifying them as broken or bad people.

REFRAMING TO CHANGE THE MEANING

When discussing teenagers who are causing their parents problems, my first reframing question is usually to ask them, "As parents, how do you distinguish between your child's rebellious behavior and the normal healthy opposition that comes when your child begins reaching for their independence?"

This question is designed to reframe the way parents view their children and their struggle. In many cases, they have never considered that a child doing something contrary to a parent's wishes could be anything but dysfunctional. This frame not only allows them a new approach to their child's behavior, but also often takes away some of the fear or shame that some parents have when facing conflict with their teenagers.

Reframing is more than just finding a silver lining. It is giving a whole new way for people to see the things they are facing or believing. When people see in a new way, they live in a new way.

STRATEGY #4
QUESTIONS

Asking questions is a time-honored technique used by rabbis and therapists. These groups are invested in getting people to think freely, rather than produce rote memorized answers.

First, and most importantly, questions must be designed to pull listeners out of their passive roles. A question with a simple one-word answer narrows the mind to a single target. A question that requires thought broadens the mind and asks for engagement. While it can be used to draw someone to a specific conclusion, it allows them to arrive at that conclusion of their own free will.

- *"Why would Jesus heal all the lepers even though He knew only one would return?"*

- This kind of question doesn't have a clear and specific answer, but it moves listeners toward the generous thought processes of the Lord. The exact answers might vary, but it allows people to congregate around a potential thought shift.

- *"How many blind people did Jesus minister to?"*

- Questions like this can disrupt thought patterns when an unexpected answer is given, such as: *"All of them. Everyone Jesus ministered to was blind."* The question shifts the meaning of "how many" from a specific number to a percentage. This shift prepares the mind for the intended shift: *"What if 'blind' has more than one meaning?"*

The point of a question is to make every engagement a conversation—not a lecture—and to engage the minds of those who listen or read. What if, like a Rabbi, you had to get all of your points across only by asking questions? How would that change your thought process? How might you see others differently?

STRATEGY #5
FACILITATION FOR ACTIVE ENGAGEMENT

Facilitation is a communication skill that moves from expressing a message to engaging your listeners in some activity. You may want your listeners to stop and imagine something or recall a memory. You may want them to engage either with each other or in some internal process.

Facilitation is an important skill for teachers who want to elicit change in their listeners because it moves people from passive listening to active engagement. The key factor that distinguishes teaching from training is that training engages students in activity and gives them the opportunity to develop a skill or experience it in the moment.

One of the most important areas of facilitation for teachers who want to elicit change is to facilitate their students in tuning in to and hearing God's voice. To stop talking *about* God and having people interact *with* God is a crucial shift to move people into meaningful, spiritual change.

Such a shift not only changes what is happening in the moment, but it has powerful, implicit messages about the ability of the student, the availability of God, and the overall meaning of discipleship. If our discipleship strategies are only learning about God in left-brained ways, then we can expect our disciples to have information about things they do not experience.

If we stop and engage them *with* God, the implicit message is clear. Discipleship involves connection to the Father.

Facilitating can be difficult for gifted teachers because it hands authority over to others in the room. Facilitating, as a skill, requires very specific and clear instructions and a willingness to stop speaking and allow others in the room to take the floor. Every facilitation has two shifts.

- The first is the shift from teaching concepts to giving instructions about the exercise.

- *"Ok, now that I have described what it is like to hear God speak, we are going to stop and practice..."*

- The second shift is from giving instructions to engaging the actual exercise.

- *"Ok, if everybody is clear on our instructions, I am about to stop speaking. When I do this, you will all begin. Ready? Begin..."*

These shifts require the teacher to give up the driver's seat and allow the students to get behind the wheel. If we want our students to be able to describe a car, then all we need to do is teach them about cars. If we want them to be safe drivers, we must relinquish the steering wheel and let them drive.

STRATEGY #6
METAPHOR

James Geary, in his brilliant book, *I Is an Other,* cites one study that found that we utter about one metaphor for every 10-25 words, or about six metaphors a minute. Metaphors connect words and meaning. Look at the example of an Australian weather forecast from Geary's book. The metaphors are in italics.

> Perth is *in the grip* of a heat wave with temperatures *set to soar* to 40 degrees Celsius by the end of the week. Australia *is no stranger* to extreme weather. Melbourne was pummeled by hailstones *the size of golf balls* on Saturday. Long term drought and bushfires *have all plagued* swathes of Queensland, New South Wales and Victoria.

Each metaphor naturally taps into imagery deeply familiar to the human experience.

Perhaps no idea could be more important in communication than understanding the use of metaphor. I have heard it said that C. S. Lewis was such an unusual thinker and theologian because he was trained in mythology and literature—not in theology. He didn't only communicate through the language of literary mechanisms, he also *thought* in the language of myth and metaphor. C.S. Lewis had unique insights into theology and the things of God because he looked into such things with a different lens.

If we think about communication as the transfer of meaning from the outside of a person's soul to the inside, we must consider that the easiest way to get meaning into someone is to attach our message to something that already has residence inside our listener.

The word metaphor comes from two Greek words and means "to carry across." A metaphor functions *to carry* meaning *across* this gap between a speaker and a listener. Metaphor is so integral to our language that it not only carries a meaning across the gap, but it also shapes thought process.

As James Geary says, "Metaphor conditions our interpretation." The use of metaphor taps into the structures already built into our listening ear and tells us how to understand what we hear.

A metaphor is like a "micro-structure" that allows words to connect with something inside listeners that is already connected to experience. Like a Trojan horse disguised as a gift, a metaphor sneaks the message behind the gates of listeners' minds and unloads the army of meaning into their city. Unsuspecting thought processes succumb to the gentle gift of a story while swallowing the meaning like medicine served up in a spoonful of sugar.

Notice how in both metaphors above, the Trojan Horse and the spoonful of sugar, the imagery is about something unwanted gaining access by tagging along with something wanted. So let's express it more positively this way: *The frosting rode in easily on the sliver of cake and was devoured with delight, creating a desire for more.*

Now aren't you hungry? The difference is subtle, but part of the power of metaphor is the subtlety of the embedded messages.

More than telling us how to interpret what we hear, metaphor can be a crucial part of the change process. Geary describes it beautifully when he says, "Metaphor systematically disorganizes the common sense of things—and reorganizes it into uncommon combinations."

The human mind operates and stores experience using the language of story. If we tell a story with a shift or unexpected ending, it helps make that shift for listeners and increases the likelihood that the listeners' minds will be shift-able.

STRATEGY #7
PARABLE

A parable is simply an extended metaphor that allows the speaker to address multiple structures in a single story. As Geary says, "Parables are narrated metaphors; they place a fictional story by the side of a fact of life." Parables allow us to engage the unconscious for a longer span as well as give the opportunity to make a shift.

Jesus tells of a Good Samaritan which is itself a shift for the Samaritan-averse audience He addressed. In a single story, He stirred up the structures related to "the desire to be seen as good," "the prejudice against a people group," "the expectation of doing God's will," and "an injured person who is helpless."

But the story arc disorganized the common sense of His audience. His listeners could not make all the structures fit together based on His telling of the story. How could they possibly replace the accepted structure that said, "Everyone knows the Samaritans are the bad guys," for a new structure that said, "The Samaritan is the hero of this story?" The uncommon ending Jesus was after was more likely accepted because He used a parable instead of a more direct approach.

You see another example when the prophet Nathan confronted David after his sin with Bathsheba and David's murder of Bathsheba's husband. Nathan came to a king who had protected and hid his misdeeds. Rather than a direct accusation, he told him a parable of a man who had many sheep but stole a sheep from another man who only had one.

Incensed that such a man might exist in his kingdom, David was prepared to bring swift justice to the scoundrel when Nathan uttered the famous words, "You are the man." Nathan's parable disorganized David's defenses and reorganized them into a new posture of receptivity.

Parables are extended metaphors. Metaphors are the shape of our thoughts, and therefore, can be used to reshape our thinking.

STRATEGY #8
CONFUSION

I have often said that Jesus' goal was to leave His listeners a bit confused. Confusion in itself was not—and is not—the goal, but it can be a great bridge to change as it is the state of a mind in flux.

The brain's primary job is to organize the world around us, which it does through structures of the mind. These provide stability, a sense of comfort and certainty, or the state of a mind that is already made up. If meaningful change is the goal, then at some point, we must ask the brain to let go of certainty so that one structure can disintegrate and a new one can be built.

If life change is the goal, it's important not to strive too hard to help people gain certainty quickly. We can introduce healthy confusion in a few ways:

- Ask a trick question,

- Make a statement that is true but disorienting,

- Or, throw a wall of words out.

Any of these will leave our listeners with looks on their faces that beg, "*What's going on?!*" In these moments, their minds are more open to change. Their structures are exposed, or possibly loosened, and what follows next has a greater chance of getting in.

For example, I like to ask the question: "Where did God hold the staff meeting when He decided to create the Heavens and the Earth?" After a pause, I follow up with the statement: "You can't answer that question because the answer would be a *place,* and God hadn't invented places yet."

These kinds of questions and statements are helpful because the mind doesn't have automatic answers. The mind stops to consider and process when assumptions are absent. Automatic answers aren't thought processes. They are default settings that automatically fill in like auto-fill on a messaging app.

I ask questions like this when I am trying to help people grasp the reality of an invisible realm. The confusion I foster here is not simply for confusion's sake. That question and statement are surprising on purpose. They expose and erode the structure known as "the nature of reality."

Confusion around the area in need of change can be a good sign. It can be like loosening the dirt near the roots of weeds that need to be pulled and breaking up the soil so new things can be planted. As such, we must use this technique wisely. God is not a God of confusion, but often His acts leave people who were once certain of their ways perplexed and pondering the truth that His ways are higher than theirs.

STRATEGY #9
UNEXPECTED WORDS

Unexpected words make people stop and think. Expected words, as just mentioned, evoke cognitive auto-fill.

One of the reasons modern translations of Scripture are so important is that words stick around well past their "sell by" date. They outlive their shelf life.

The distance between words and their meanings increases over time. If words detach from their meanings but we continue to use expected words, the resident power of those words disintegrate.

Unexpected words do not have to be words with "shock value." They can simply be words used in unusual ways. I sometimes use prefixes and suffixes where they don't belong in an effort to say something that is difficult, but necessary, to express. Examples might be:

- *"I am trying to express Jesus' incarnation-ness."*

- *"He is our source of alive-ness."*

- *"Adam was a bit creation-ish and a bit Divine-ish."*

The use of words that are incorrect (not really words) or simply uncommon words, causes the mind to stop, examine, and even consider. Remember the processes of deletion, generalization, and distortion from Chapter Five? Unexpected words or phrases allow ideas to pierce through the filtration system.

The point here is not simply to be clever, but to stop the mind on the concepts that need attention. The mind prefers efficiency, and new ways of learning are not always efficient. Keys to this technique are:

- Use words that make the mind stop and examine.

- Be intentional.

- Take time to examine and select words that prove unexpected to even the speaker.

STRATEGY #10
IMPLICATION

Implication is a powerful tool that presumes the unconscious mind is learning all the time. Indirect statements or suggestions allow the mind to come to its own conclusions. The power of an implication is that it takes the first several steps in a direction, assuming that the mind will finish the journey under its own steam.

Implication can be a general idea like: "Whether the change happens this week or in two months, you will be amazed at how much better you feel."

The general implication is that the change *is* going to come, and it could be fairly soon.

Implication can also be more specific: "Whether you do this exercise with your eyes open or with your eyes closed, it will still work. You pick which is most comfortable."

The clear implication here is that you are going to do the exercise. The choice offered makes it sound like you are completely free to do whatever you please. The parameters given overtly (eyes open or eyes closed) keep you from noticing the directive given covertly (do this exercise).

One of my favorite moments that demonstrates the power of implication to shift a conversation is found in Matthew 17:24-27. Jesus' disciples are confronted with the question about whether or not Jesus paid taxes to the Roman government.

Jesus questioned Peter about who taxes are collected from and then made the greatest statement ever.

"Go get a fish!" He said. He then told Peter to open the fish's mouth and take out the coin to pay the tax in question.

Don't miss the brilliance of the moment. One commentary said this was one of Jesus' least dramatic miracles. I disagree. The nature of the argument was about how Jesus related to the governing structures of Rome. Jesus gave a non-dramatic instruction to go catch a fish, open its mouth and remove the exact change to pay the temple tax from that fish.

Watch what He "said" without using a word.

Question: *"How does your master Jesus relate to the government of the nation of Rome?"*

Answer: *"However He pleases. Clearly He relates to an entirely different and higher government that can find tax payments in a not-so-random fish."*

In pure implication, Jesus changed the entire conversation by making a clear demonstration that He runs the universe. The rest of the conversation had to matter very little compared to how it began.

STRATEGY #11
HUMOR

Humor is like confusion only more fun. Humor provides a loosening of the normal defenses and, done well, creates an openness. It is very helpful as a rapport-builder when you are in a new setting.

Here are a few suggestions for using humor effectively:

- Humor must be appropriate to the environment.

- Humor does not always translate well. Don't expect your joke to work when working with a translator. Humor is typically based on culture and/or language usage.

- Humor should be used sparingly as too much humor suggests that the speaker does not take themselves or their topic seriously.

- Humor should never be self-deprecating. This kind of humor detracts from the message and undermines the speaker's credibility.

The ideal use of humor is when the punch line makes a shift in thought or expectation, particularly in the targeted area of change.

STRATEGY #12
THOUGHT INTERRUPTION

Thought interruption can be done from a platform or within a dialogue. Both can be effective. Thought interruption is based on the idea that thoughts run together in predictable sequences and are likely to complete their own sequence if not interrupted.

Much like unconsciously singing the lyrics to a song, the mind will complete its own train of thought without any conscious effort. When in dialogue, if you pay attention to the language of the other person, they will begin to reveal their assumptions. They don't know they are assumptions—or lies—until we question them.

When someone reveals a lie they believe, we can look for a simple opportunity to plant a question mark. It isn't necessary or advisable to oppose or correct the lie as the mind has strategies to resist that kind of input. By planting a question mark, the mind will stop to consider the answer.

For example, someone says, "I am analytical."

You may respond, "Are you sure?"

They say, "Of course, I am."

You respond again, "Is that who you are, or just a habit you have learned?"

Generally, at this point, they will reconsider their statement.

Or, someone might say, "I am just lazy."

You respond, "What if you're not?"

Often you get one more chance as they counter, "But, I am!"

We can go back to identity versus behavior and ask, "Is it who you are, or just what you have seen yourself do recently?"

Strategies for using this technique include:

- Asking short, direct questions and allowing for silence to follow.

- Not giving opposition or correction.

- After interrupting the train of thought allow them to process without your input.

The process of asking a short, direct question followed by expectant silence stops the train of thought and invites a chasm where new thoughts can occur.

From a platform, the approach is different but can be equally effective. Since you can't hear the audience's words, it is helpful to know something of their culture or typical thought processes. The thought interruption can be an unusual phrase or a mildly controversial statement that catches the attention of listeners.

Here's an example I like using: "You may have been told your whole life that you are supposed to live for God. What if I told you that you were never supposed to live for God?"

Then pause and read the room. "It was never the design of the human soul that we live *for* God. We were designed to live *from* God."

This direct challenge to a broad assumption is a thought-stopper.

Stopping a train of thought creates a moment of "thought vacuum." In that gap, where the train of thought has stopped and not started back up again, there is a wonderful state of potential change waiting for your next words.

The mind already has momentum so when you stop the train of thought and drop something into the gap, the momentum of the mind can pick up the new idea.

STRATEGY #13
CHANGE THOUGHT PROCESSES

So often we attempt to help people have new thoughts, but by now you know that thoughts are subject to already existing thought *processes.*

If you help people change their thought *process,* then further change is inevitable.

In Chapter Five, we talked about how the mind lifts a teaspoon of data from the sand-filled beach of input. The mind regularly focuses on some things while screening out other things that it has ignored or distorted for years. Out of millions of data bits assailing the senses, only 126 bits of data will sink in. The 126 bits of data that make it into our consciousness are screened by our pre-existing structures.

Our job is to show the mind something new right in the middle of the old. We must question the mind's selection and question why it has chosen those particular 126 bits. We must interrupt our listeners' thought processes.

If your listeners always see the gorilla, then point out the basketball. If they only see the basketball, draw them to the excruciating details of the gorilla. Ask them what another person might be experiencing.

Find any way you can to help them see the limitations of seeing and know the limitations of knowing. If they see 126 completely new bits, they will have doubled their perspective.

Consider these thought process shifts. You can help people move from:

RECITE → IMPROVISE

MEMORIZE → SYNTHESIZE

CONCRETE → ABSTRACT

REASON → INTUITION

LITERAL LEARNING → INFERENTIAL LEARNING

CONTENT LEVEL → META LEVEL

FOCUS → PERIPHERAL

LEFT HEMISPHERE → RIGHT HEMISPHERE

Let's look at these one by one.

RECITE → IMPROVISE

Most people have learned to memorize and recite. This is the default definition of learning for the average Western thinker because this method will make students successful at school. Improvisation is a thought process that requires the learning of primary knowledge but then moves beyond that to spontaneous composition.

Improvisation is the flow of spontaneous thought and action derived from information stored in the mind. Rather than a recitation of this information, improvisation allows for a stream-of-awareness thought process to create or deviate in mid-stream.

Improvisation draws from a pool of learned ideas or concepts and allows a spontaneous flow of these ideas to be created on the spot. Rather than reciting memorized ideas, a learner is encouraged to re-organize their ideas to express something personal. It requires learned ideas, but encourages a personalized synthesis and expression of those ideas.

Improvisation in music shifts the learning process from a "memorization-to-playing-to-hearing" process to a "hearing-internally-to-playing" process. It is a completely different thought process that requires an internal shift and produces something new or different every time.

MEMORIZE → SYNTHESIZE

Before you can improvise, you must learn to synthesize. Whether you improvise in music, speaking, comedy, or sports, you must first learn to combine learned concepts into new concepts or combinations of concepts. This is a required shift to be able to improvise. Taking stored information and developing connections and interactions between the data is the first shift in higher-level thinking.

Teachers must see themselves as stimulants to change rather than merchants of data. We can help people go beyond what a teacher provides and consider combinations or interactions of resident knowledge to come up with original ideas. When we combine ideas, every idea is greater than the sum of its parts.

We can extend invitations of creativity to our audiences. We can encourage them to be like the musician who is limited to a finite number of notes, but unlimited in the way he combines those notes. We can encourage them to take limited ideas and combine or vary them.

I watched a young child, his first year in basketball, run the plays his coach had taught him. When the flow shifted, he continued to run the same exact patterns he had been shown. No one bothered to tell him he needed to interact with the game; they had only told him to run the plays. He had memorized, but never synthesized.

CONCRETE → ABSTRACT

Moving from concrete to abstract is easier for some people than others. It is a crucial step because it moves the mind from rigid to flexible. "Concrete" is a word with very specific meaning. It sets in place and resists change and flexibility. A concrete thinker often doesn't even realize that abstract thought is possible while abstract thinkers understand both.

It takes abstract communication to move people away from concrete thought and it often frustrates people and produces confusion. This must be pushed through. Like Jesus teaching in parables and refusing to cater to an incompatible thought process, a teacher must be willing to tear down the idol of thought process.

REASON → INTUITION

The thought processes of reason and intuition are "ways of knowing." Both are valid. Reason takes in concrete data and tries to provide logical connections and implications. Intuition responds to less observable input and synthesizes it through subtle connections. Often the process of intuition looks a little mystical because it is less able to be observed and proven. Nonetheless, it is a valid and accurate way of knowing.

However, various "ways of knowing" produce varied "*knowings*." You cannot know about love through reason, and you cannot know about engineering through intuition.

We must help people develop both. If we, as speakers, are not very intuitive, it will be difficult for us to foster these thought processes in other people. Intuition is usually something we need to teach people to *trust* more than learn. Intuitive learning or thinking is usually present, but many dismiss it. The more we can teach people to trust it, the more they become aware of what is already present.

LITERAL LEARNING → INFERENTIAL LEARNING

Literal learning refers to observing and memorizing data without drawing conclusions. Information is information. Inferential learning is the process of learning the covert messages or meanings in communication.

A literal learner asks the question, "Did you just say…?"

An inferential learner asks, "Did you mean…?"

It is important that you as a speaker develop both types of learning. People tend to be stronger in one form or the other. Learn to recognize which one is stronger in you and work to develop the other.

The rabbinical style of teaching—use of metaphor, questions, and object lessons—strengthens the inferential style of learning. As with all the shifts in this section, the move to inferential learning allows more of the learner's person to be involved in the learning process.

CONTENT LEVEL → META LEVEL

Meta-perspectives are overarching or seeing the larger context. Helping people learn to think from a meta-perspective is invaluable. We must teach people to "view from above" or "from outside" a conversation. Meta-thinking is the ability to *think about thinking* or to *learn about learning*.

Meta-perspectives always make you look wiser because you can respond from either outside or inside a conversation.

One person might say, "You are almost out of money."

One response would be, "I know it looks like it, but I have more in another account."

A meta-response would be, "It seems that you keep a pretty close eye on me."

Someone with a meta-perspective doesn't respond *to* the conversation; they respond *about* the conversation.

A teacher who intends to stimulate thought must talk about talking, think about thinking, and teach about teaching. These all provide a meta-perspective and allow for a greater level of perception and understanding.

Meta-thinking is also the basis of empathy. To empathize with another requires the capacity to view from a perspective other than your own.

FOCUS → PERIPHERAL

The unconscious mind is a powerful mechanism of learning. Because it has fewer filters, the unconscious mind can take in more information in a given moment. It also takes in a different kind of information.

Focused learning has a target, whereas peripheral learning has a scope. Focused learning leads to reason, whereas peripheral learning leads to intuitive thinking.

FOCUSED LEARNING → TARGET: REASON

PERIPHERAL LEARNING → SCOPE: INTUITIVE THINKING

Focused learning can create tension. Peripheral learning can release tension. Often people with testing anxiety only know focused learning and have not learned how to trust that their mind is wired to learn. Peripheral learning is the reason that so many professional educators decorate the learning environment with visuals and other reminders of the concepts in a lesson or series.

This idea can actually be introduced as a way to overtly shift the way your listeners receive. You can even suggest that they shift to a different way of receiving.

When I speak in church settings, I often follow a worship set, or a time of music intended to engage a congregation. When I step up to the platform, I can feel the room begin to shift. As they are pulling out notebooks or bibles, they are shifting to a mode of "focused learning."

I often ask the people to stop a moment and notice the shift. I ask them to stay in the same state they were in before the shift. For those who can, it noticeably increases their receptivity.

For a moment, look at this word: FOCUS

Pay attention to the word and attune your thoughts and senses to it. Notice how you experience this.

Now look at this word: PERIPHERAL

This time, as you look also notice what else is happening in the environment around you. Hear the sounds and see the room you are in. You still take in the word, but how do you experience it differently?

LEFT HEMISPHERE → RIGHT HEMISPHERE

Many of the strategies recommended in this section fall under this umbrella. While we spent all of Chapter Seven learning about this, it still matters as we discuss techniques to facilitate change. We must remember that mind speaks to mind, but hemisphere also speaks to hemisphere.

If you want people to memorize information, you can simply feed them information. If you want them to have a response, connect to the concepts, or experience change, you must shoot for the right hemisphere of the brain.

The list of strategies for this is in Chapter Seven, but keep in mind that a right-brained approach is a way of thinking and not just a set of techniques. Those techniques should spur the way of thinking—not be a substitute for it.

Perhaps I should say it this way:

The little ones felt the excitement in the air. Even their teachers seemed a bit lighter with anticipation. This was the day they all loved. This was the day that the Rabbi came to *their* class. They all knew that his time was important. They all knew he knew things they did not.

The door opened, and he hurried in with a grocery bag tucked under his arm. Immediately their curiosity was piqued. What did he bring today?

He reached in the bag and began to remove a stack of squares cut from wax paper. Smiling and humming while greeting some of the students by name, he handed out one square to each student.

Next he pulled a squeeze bottle of honey from the bag. He went down the row and squeezed a few drops onto each child's square of wax paper. As he went, he looked each one of them in the eyes, held up his finger as if to say "wait" and moved on.

When he had given each child a few drops of the golden liquid, he opened up the Scriptures.

"Psalm 34:8," he said and then he paused.

Slowly, with a twinkle in his eye, he looked around the room. He saw them look at him and then at their wax paper. He felt their excitement bump up a notch.

"Who knows what it says?" he asked his increasingly distracted pupils.

Some raised their hands, some raised their waxed paper.

"Shimon?" he prompted. "Tell us slowly."

They young man beamed, looked down at his waxed paper and began with the words.

"Taste…and…see…"

Several of the students raised the honey to their lips.

The Rabbi nodded and with a gesture invited them all to continue.

"That…the…Lord…" The sound of kids licking waxed paper began to spread across the room.

"Is…good…"

"Mmmmm mmmmm," the sound rose spontaneously from the students.

BONUS: FOUR SELF-STRATEGIES FOR CHANGING YOU, THE COMMUNICATOR

As a communicator implementing new strategies, it can be easy to fall into a place where your teaching becomes rote and ordinary, full of repetition—and suddenly becomes anything *but* soul-changing. Here are a few strategies I like to keep in mind for myself as a speaker that will also benefit you.

SELF-STRATEGY #1:
SHIFT FROM INITIATOR TO RECEIVER

In the Garden of Eden, we changed from receivers (He blew into the man's nostrils the breath of life) to initiators (He picked from the tree leaves to cover his nakedness). Man was designed to receive, contain, and then broadcast the Breath of Life. The Knowledge of Good and Evil has made us people who try to live by knowing and doing. We ask these questions:

- What should we do *for* God?

- How should we live *for* God?

What if instead we return to our created design and learn to live *from* God?

When we make the shift from initiator to receiver, we position ourselves to wait and listen. Striving and effort are signs that we are trying to initiate. When we are at rest, still on the inside, we can better hear and sense the movement of God's Spirit toward us.

As we grow in our ability to sense God's movement and His voice, we become more like a boat driven by a sail than by a motor. We wait on the wind, we catch it in our mind, and we allow it to move us.

Rest is the posture, and rest is the result.

We must learn to make the shift from Hear-Reason-Do to Receive-Contain-Broadcast.

SELF-STRATEGY #2:
CHANGE YOUR MOTIVE

Changing our motive when addressing an audience changes everything. Our motive must change from anything we do to satisfy or soothe selfish needs to the motive of seeing and connecting to others. Often our selfish needs lie just below the surface. Consider the kinds of responses you are hoping for—or the disappointment you feel if they don't come.

Do you need validation? "Good job, Bob, you were really spot on today!"

Do you need admiration? "That was incredible! You are such a good communicator!"

If people don't give that kind of feedback, do you find yourself bothered? Do you, at some level, rely on the responses of others to believe you have succeeded?

Of course it's important to read a room or notice visual cues from an audience. That is different than getting your emotional needs tangled up in your speaking. I am talking about the kind of emotional experience you have if you don't get a certain kind of feedback. If you are frustrated, disappointed, or insecure without positive feedback, you might have selfish, emotional needs connected to your speaking.

One way you might notice this is if you ask the audience to respond or react as a way to manage your discomfort. Direct requests for specific kinds of feedback can indicate your emotions are on the line. It can also potentially insult your audience.

Consider that connection alone is a value and an important motive. Consider that the people in front of you are supposed to benefit in some way from what you have given them. If you are trying to help them change, be careful that your expectations or needs don't put unnecessary pressure on your audience.

SELF-STRATEGY #3:
TEACH WITH IMMEDIACY

Picture yourself standing before your listeners and describing for two minutes what "cold" is.

Now imagine doing it again after leaving your hand buried in a bucket of ice for two minutes.

Imagine the difference! The idea is that whatever you teach can be taught from *immediacy*. Immediacy means to teach from a current experience by focusing on an idea and letting the words follow.

This can work by bringing any idea, picture, or concept to mind. Picture it. Let yourself experience it. Now describe what you see. Take the time to explore the idea and let words come *in the moment*.

Can you feel the difference in your own experience if you start with the idea first and let the words come second? It's the difference between describing the concept of cold and relating the experience of leaving your hand in ice. The second—teaching from the experience—has the power to draw in your listeners and take them on a journey with you.

SELF-STRATEGY #4:
SAY IT ANOTHER WAY

Another way I like to pry myself out of repetition and recitation is to look for multiple ways to say the same thing, If I can say it more than one way— and then more than two ways—I will break myself out of stale words and into using fresh ones.

Or, let me say this another way.

If we have taught the same idea more than once, we shouldn't give ourselves the luxury of repeating phrases. We should try to say the same ideas but with brand new words.

Or, let me say it another way.

Just because our words have made sense to us, we should try a few different ways to say the same thing in case our listeners need to hear it differently than we do.

FINAL THOUGHTS ON THESE TOOLS

My preference and my belief are that if I help *you* think in a new way, then you will figure out how that translates into new ways of doing. I told a friend recently that in his situation he didn't need any new techniques; he needed a whole new view of his circumstances.

Part of the value of this belief is that it honors those who listen or read and believes in their ability to think and reason. While many people just want concrete answers, the mind craves the freedom to explore and leave the bounds of learning as defined by listening and memorizing.

We can use these tools freely and creatively. We can learn to bend them and combine them, learn to synthesize elements of the old ways and generate completely new ways that rise up from inside our unique designs. We can use these tools, not allowing them to sit in the garage and gather dust. Instead, we can pull them out regularly and enjoy the power of our communication to minds that will listen.

Now, let's go and play!

STUDY GUIDE

KEY CONCEPTS

- There are countless ways to shift people's beliefs. This chapter is your tool box.

- There are tools you can use not only for helping your listeners, but also for helping yourself as a communicator.

SKILL BUILDERS

1. Pick one skill each day this week to practice in conversations.

2. Do you have an area of your life where you can learn to improvise? If so begin to practice this. If not, begin to search for a way to develop this thought process.

3. Consider your motive when teaching. How can you reframe your approach?

4. Have fun, be creative and go play!

CONCLUSION

"How many therapists does it take to change a light bulb?"

The answer?

"It only takes one, but the light bulb must really want to change."

Embedded in the joke is the age-old question: *Who is responsible for change?* The truth is that each individual is responsible for changing himself or herself. Each of us is responsible for changing ourselves.

Over the years, I have observed that far more people struggle to change because they are tied in knots as opposed to remaining unmoved by a stubborn unwillingness.

The goal of this book has been to assist you as you help others experience meaningful change. This is a sacred call. It allows us to enter into the lives of our listeners and offer them an invitation to a new life, to show them a road less traveled, a path previously hidden from their sight. And with the information and techniques you have learned in this book, you are better prepared to invite them to rise from the ashes of an old life or see a specific topic in a whole new way.

As someone who has spent his professional life working with people searching for change, I can tell you these moments are, indeed, sacred. Our words and our ability to use them adequately and reverently are all we have. They can allow us to cross over the gap between us, reach the deep places of our fellow man, and invite them to bring themselves to the forefront. It's a privilege to be part of that journey.

And finally, it is my hope that in these pages you have also found your own self, as you have discovered the power of communication and discovered the *common union* among us all. I hope you have discovered that while your mind and your being are brilliant, they are not so complex that you too cannot come out and play.

Before we end our time together, I encourage you to complete one last assignment. Return to Chapter One and reread "Learning to Fly," the Parable of the Acrobat.

- How does this story read differently now that you have gained greater understanding about words and learning?

- How are the principles you've learned in this book evident in the story?

- Ask God how you can put this book's principles and techniques to use to better serve the people He sends to you—the people He loves.

And of course, I'd love to hear about your successes. Drop me a line at BobHamp.com or leave a review on Amazon so I can celebrate with you and hear what this book has meant to you. You may also connect with me on Facebook at fb.com/TheBobHamp or send me a tweet @bobhamp.

Always remember, your mind and the minds of those in your audience are brilliant. They don't even have to ask for permission to be so. But with permission and intentionality, you and your audience can discover that by thinking differently, you can learn differently, and if you learn differently, then the mysteries of the Kingdom and the cosmos are at your fingertips.

REFERENCES

Anderson, Neil T. *Victory over the Darkness: Realize the Power of Your Identity in Christ*. Minneapolis: Bethany House, 2000.

Bandler, Richard, and John Grinder. *The Structure of Magic: A Book about Language and Therapy*. Palo Alto: Science and Behavior Books, 1975.

Dilts, Robert B. *Changing Belief Systems with NLP*. Meta Publications, 1990.

Brown, B. (2012, March) Brené Brown: Listening to Shame [Video file]. Retrieved from "www.ted.com/talks/brene_brown_listening_to_shame."

Efran, Jay S., Michael D. Lukens, and Robert J. Lukens. *Language, Structure, and Change: Frameworks of Meaning in Psychotherapy*. New York: W. W. Norton and Company, 1990.

Farber, Adele, and Elaine Mazlish. *How to Talk so Kids Will Listen and Listen so Kids Will Talk*. New York: Scribner (Negotiation Institute), 1980.

Geary, James. *I is An Other: The Secret Life of Metaphor and How it Shapes the Way We See the World*. New York: Harper Perennial. 2011

Hamp, Bob. *Think Differently Live Differently: Keys to a Life of Freedom*. (2nd ed.). Grapevine: Thinking Differently Press, 2010-2016

Newberg, Andrew, Eugene D'Aquill, and Vance Rouse. *Why God Won't Go Away: Brain Science and the Biology of Belief*. New York: Ballantine Books, 2001.

ALSO BY BOB HAMP

Think Differently Live Differently: Keys to a Life of Freedom
Now is a good time to become yourself, to discover your God-created, God-connected true self. Now is a good time to *Think Differently* about things that ruled your life.

Think Differently Lead Differently: Bringing Reformation in Your Heart, Your Home and Your Organization
Reexamine long-held assumptions about leadership in the Kingdom and go about your high calling in fresh ways. Whether you're currently endeavoring to lead a reformation in your organization, your family, or simply your own heart, you'll find this book a powerful and eye-opening guide.

Think Differently Lead Differently **DVD training series**
"Go deeper" in this life-changing video series based on the book.

Foundations of Freedom **DVD training series**
Have you ever felt that you were not living the life that God designed for you to live? If we do not first change the way we think, even new thoughts will follow old pathways. This series is designed to shift thought processes, allowing old ideas to take on new meaning.

Visit BobHamp.com

ABOUT THE AUTHOR

Bob Hamp is an author, speaker, and teacher proclaiming the freedom offered through the gospel. Coming from an unchurched background, he was unexpectedly ambushed by an encounter with God that changed the direction and foundation of his life forever. His unique slant on the Gospel is the result of looking through the lens of a counselor and sitting across from people in need for almost three decades.

Licensed as a Marriage and Family Therapist in Texas, Bob was in private practice for 16 years, helping people with every type of struggle imaginable. He then stepped into one of the fastest-growing churches in Texas, where he spent nine years developing a discipleship strategy called Freedom Ministry.

Now, Bob and his wife Polly are the Owners and Directors of Think Differently Counseling, Coaching and Connecting; a counseling and training center in Grapevine, Texas. Specializing in freedom based counseling and coaching. They offer topical classes, training events and a Think Differently Training Certification program. Together they feel called to make disciples without building a congregation.

Bob and Polly have six grown kids, four grandchildren, and two corgis.

BobHamp.com | facebbook.com/TheBobHamp | @bobhamp